JANET MALCOLM

JANET MALCOLM
THE LAST INTERVIEW
and OTHER CONVERSATIONS

with an introduction by KATIE ROIPHE

MELVILLE HOUSE
BROOKLYN · LONDON

Melville House Publishing   Suite 2000
          46 John Street and 16/18 Woodford Road
        Brooklyn, NY 11201   London E7 0HA

mhpbooks.com
@melvillehouse

ISBN: 978-1-61219-968-9
ISBN: 978-1-61219-969-9 (ebook)

Printed in the United States of America

1 3 5 7 9 10 8 6 4 2

A catalog record for this book is available from the Library of Congress.

CONTENTS

INTRODUCTION

KATIE ROIPHE

When a friend texted me that Janet Malcolm had died, I experienced more than the usual amount of disbelief. Even after all these years of knowing her, I had not totally absorbed the idea of her as ordinarily mortal. Though she had told me about her lung cancer, and though she had looked quite frail the last time I had seen her, she did not seem like someone who could die.

I've noticed that Janet has always aroused extreme responses of veneration or suspicion among journalists and writers. Those journalists that don't fervently admire her tend to be bristly about her, morally disapproving of her methods of quotation. Jealousy, it always seemed to me. The resentment that attaches to the transcendently talented from the merely functional. After her libel trial with Jeffrey Masson, which shadowed her life for a decade, she wrote about herself as "a kind of fallen woman of journalism," but she was also one of its stars.

For some reason, a looming part of Malcolm's reputation is that she was cold, brutal. Even an admiring critic classifies her as a reporter "given to mutilating her subjects." In a purely descriptive *New York Times* piece, she is "a master of pitiless prose" and an "austere, driven woman." In her *New York Times* obituary, one critic is quoted as saying, "Don't ever eat in front of Janet Malcolm; or show her your apartment; or cut tomatoes while she watches."

In her lifetime I did not think to question this widely held view of her as austere or cold or pitiless, but now I wonder about it.

Janet herself did not connect with the image of herself as scary or brutal. I first met her in her Gramercy Park apartment when I did an interview with her for *The Paris Review*. She liked the introduction that I wrote to the interview, in which I confessed my fear of her judgments or analysis of me when I first met her, but she wrote, "Am I as forbidding as that???" Of course she wasn't. In person she was nice. She was enormously interested in other people, sympathetic, unusually supportive. What was forbidding was the rigorous intellectual universe she had created, the standards she had laid down for other writers. What was intimidating was the beauty in the sentences.

The reputation for coldness arose from her work. But did "brutal" actually just mean "good"? Was she perceived as harsh because she looked very closely at people, observed on a superior plane, and could wring from ordinary happenings more refined and precise meanings than other practitioners of the craft? As one of my undergraduates put it, "She's like a psychoanalyst freed from the need to heal people."

The artist David Salle, one of her subjects who evolved into a close friend, questioned the idea of Janet as cold: "I think Janet's reputation for cool detachment was misplaced. You can be empathetic and a realist about human nature at the same time . . . She had a deep reservoir of sympathy for anyone engaged in the struggle to be human—she couldn't have written those pieces without it."

And this seems fundamentally true. The critics and journalists who view Janet as cold are missing a vital part of her project, as it manifested over the years: the bright strain of generosity, the effort to dive deep into motivation, to understand others on the highest level. Her idea that the production of official narratives is suspect, that narratives are created by flawed individuals, in ways she proceeds to expose, is, at its core, respectful of the mysteries and complexities and intricacies of human life.

I think it is important to note that this view of Malcolm's work as brutal, by women as well as men, may be gendered. There may be something about a woman dismantling personal mythologies and delving brilliantly into motivations that irks or riles us. One critic referred to her "not-niceness." But male writers with the gift of cutting through people's delusions and pretensions are not labelled "cold" or "not-nice." I think here of writers like James Baldwin and Christopher Hitchens, who tend to be admired as truth tellers rather than "cold" or "brutal." This is one of the conversations I wish I'd had with Janet herself at Choshi, the now-closed sushi place she favored around the corner from her house. I know she would have had thoughts on it.

It's a bit odd to think of writing about Janet for a book of her interviews, since she disliked them generally and did so few of them, and then often with ground rules and reluctance. She only agreed to do my *Paris Review* interview via email, as she did with *The Believer*, so she could mull over and write her answers and retain maximal control. She could not really stomach the idea of another journalist wielding a recording device and her helplessly talking into it. In her *Salon* interview, she offers one explanation of her aversion: "I'm just not very good at it. I often have no answers to the questions; I think of the answers later." Though one doubts that she was not "very good" at anything to do with words, she did not like the impromptu or spontaneous, in part because she took questions, like everything else, more seriously than other people. She did not toss off answers. She wanted to consider things from every angle. As she put it in her testimony during her first jury trial: "This thing called speech is sloppy, redundant, repetitious, full of *uhs* and *ahs*." To her, speech required trimming and shaping. Consequently, her interviews are well wrought, careful, considered, in a way that other people's aren't. Other people are accepting of a kind of casualness and mediocrity of expression that Janet never was, in any arena of life.

This particular feeling about speech—that it should represent the best of its speaker—carried through into her work itself. In her pieces, she famously curated her subject's speech, piecing together quotes from various interviews and settings so that they would be at their most articulate. That they would be most themselves. This was, of course, a highly controversial tactic, but she was, in her estimation, presenting them most truthfully and fairly. In editing interviews together, she was achieving a more natural effect of their speech and personality. About cutting and pasting quotes in her writing on Masson, she said, "I needed to present it in logical, rational order so he would sound like a logical, rational person."

Perhaps another reason Janet disliked interviews is that the idea of displaying or revealing herself seemed somehow a little bit vulgar. She never said this to me directly, but I gleaned this attitude from her response to other people's public personas. In my own interview, I could feel her subtly and sometimes not so subtly shift the topic from more personal questions to matters of craft. She sometimes said things like, "Let's change the subject." When I asked her about whether she ever experienced a conflict between writing and motherhood, she said, "This may be too deep a subject for an email exchange on the art of nonfiction. Probably the place to discuss our struggles with the art of mothering is a dark bar." Needless to say, we never made it to that dark bar.

Janet was very private. She was so private that, when someone wrote a villanelle in *Harper's Magazine* about our interview and referenced a giant mirror in her living room, she was spooked. How did the poet know she had a giant, ornate mirror? Had I communicated with him? We had several conversations on this topic. I suggested this was not that distinctive a detail, and he must have guessed or made it up. But it felt for a moment like important matters of state were being accessed by an enemy power. It was bothering her so much that I asked her if I should write to the poet and ask him. She said I should, so I did. He wrote back: "I've never been in Janet's apartment! I made the mirror up! Is there a mirror? Is it ornate? The plot thickens."

She disliked anything that romanticized or rendered grandiose the role of the writer. When I asked her if she viewed writing as cabinetmaking or something more mystical, she very adamantly chose cabinetmaking. She studiously avoided sentimental ideas of the writer's specialness. She mischievously enjoyed puncturing people's pretentious expectations. I love her response when *The New York Times* reporter asked her what books were on her nightstand, expecting her to say something like *The Death of Ivan Illych* or some obscure Eastern European psychoanalytic tract, and instead she said, "A box of Kleenex, a two-year-old Garnet Hill catalog and a cough drop on it." That was very Janet.

In the course of my interview with her, Janet made several comments that gestured toward the possibility that she was merely human. I fixate on something she tells me about being unsure about what to bring to the house of one of her subjects on a Jewish holiday. She picks a bag of kosher cookies, thinks they look cheap, contemplates exchanging them for chocolate bark, and then is distracted through the evening by the question of whether her host will serve them. It is impossible to connect Janet, as I understand her, with this moment of ordinary insecurity, this totally mundane instance of doubt. I think of her moving through that world with absolute confidence. I think the confidence in the sentences is in her life.

I have always used her writing to teach confidence to students. We try to break down the question of authority, how it works on the page. We look at Janet's work, how her interpretations seem to rise organically out of her descriptions, the utter naturalness and mastery of her authority. To deconstruct confidence, to break down its effect, is like trying to deconstruct a magic trick, and yet year after year we do it.

At the end of the semester, my students, colleagues, and I have a big party with a cake. One particularly artistic student has printed out photographs of the writers we admire and cut their faces out in circles and put them on Popsicle sticks on the cake, and of course, there is Janet, her serious bespectacled face rising out of the rainbow sprinkled icing. When it's time to slice it onto paper plates, I hear the students jostling over who gets Janet.

I love the reverential hush that descends on the first day of the semester when I read the description of Rosalind Krauss's loft from "A Girl of the Zeitgeist." I love seeing the paperbacks of *The Silent Woman* or *In the Freud Archives* emerging from the backpacks of another generation of students. I love when one of them quotes aloud to the class a passage they have highlighted and marked up in their Bushwick bedroom. She is still here. She is still with us.

JANET MALCOLM

THE JOURNALIST AND THE PROVOCATEUR

INTERVIEW BY NAN GOLDBERG
SALON
NOVEMBER 28, 2001

Janet Malcolm has reason to be gun-shy. A brilliant essayist whose best work has parsed the unstated contradictions inherent in psychoanalysis, journalism and the law, Malcolm endured a decade-long libel lawsuit (1984 to 1994) by psychoanalyst Jeffrey Masson, who accused her of fabricating quotes in her 1984 book about him, *In the Freud Archives*. (A judge dismissed the suit, but Masson appealed and the case eventually went to a jury, which found for Malcolm.)

During the years of the lawsuit and even afterward, Malcolm was routinely represented by the press as an example of bad, unethical journalism. Masson's accusations had found a receptive audience among some of Malcolm's fellow journalists, perhaps because of her propensity for bluntly stating awkward truths that others prefer to leave unsaid and perhaps even unacknowledged. Pondering her own profession, for example, she famously began *The Journalist and the Murderer* (1990): "Every journalist who is not too stupid or too full of himself to notice what is going on knows that what he does is morally indefensible. He is a kind of confidence man, preying on people's vanity, ignorance, or loneliness, gaining their trust and betraying them without remorse."

Happily for her, Malcolm's new book, *Reading Chekhov*, is unlikely to offend anyone. Part biography, part literary criticism, it is a typical Malcolm work in its hybrid, montage-like nature. And yet it is a departure, too: Its subject is dead, for one thing, and the book does not, like most of her work, attempt to weave together a complete narrative, with a beginning, middle and end, out of interviews, research and common sense. Rather, Malcolm says, she simply wanted to understand the power of Chekhov's masterful stories.

Salon visited with Malcolm recently at her Manhattan apartment.

NAN GOLDBERG: Given what you wrote in *The Journalist and the Murderer* about the journalist-subject relationship—that it's a power relationship and the power is all in the journalist's hands—why did you agree to be interviewed?

JANET MALCOLM: It's a very good question. At the time [I wrote that book], I did not do any interviews. When the book came out and people wanted to ask me questions, I said, "Well, read the book."

GOLDBERG: I did. That's why I'm asking.

MALCOLM: But time goes on . . . And one of the reasons I did not give interviews, of course, was not just the power in this. I'm just not very good at it. I often have no answers to the questions; I think of the answers later.

I also feel I've already said what I want to say in my work. So the questions are asking me to think about things that either I've already thought about and set down there, or if the question is a new question, I can't just answer it right off the bat because the answer won't be interesting.

GOLDBERG: In Chekhov's "A Dreary Story," the narrator at the end realizes that he lacks a ruling idea from which to make sense of his existence. In your work, on the other hand, it's clear you center around certain problems, or a series of related problems.

MALCOLM: Yes, we all do the same things over again, the repetition compulsion. [You don't think you're starting out] with some ruling idea, but as you go along you realize that you keep coming back to the same subject.

GOLDBERG: What Philip Roth talks about over and over again in his work is how we can't know each other, that we keep getting it wrong: We get it wrong and we get it wrong again, and then we think about it and try again and get it wrong again. And that seems to me what you are trying to get at also: What's true? Is it possible to know what's true? But I'd really like to hear you describe what your work is about.

MALCOLM: I'd love to hear you talk about it rather than me. See, you're thinking like a critic. Writers don't always care to write in the kind of consciousness in which criticism is conducted. They would be paralyzed, too aware of what they're doing. I really think it's for the critic to try to figure out what's going on.

That's what's delighted me so much about this [Chekhov] book. I've really enjoyed figuring out what it is that makes his

stories what they are. I read them over and over, and each time
I read one of his stories—always, it was a new experience. I
would always reach a point where my eyes would start tearing;
here it would come again—extraordinary.

GOLDBERG: What drew you to Chekhov particularly?

MALCOLM: I'd read some Chekhov, the plays and some stories, and then a few years ago Ecco Press started publishing
his stories, and I started reading them and falling in love
with them.

    James Atlas was doing this series called Penguin Lives,
and he called me up and asked if I would do a biography. I
didn't think I had any interest in writing a biography, so I
said, "I'm sorry," but he asked me to think about it and then
he called again, and I thought, all right, I'll do Chekhov.

    Actually I think I'd already tried to do a little writing
about these stories, which are so mysteriously wonderful.

GOLDBERG: How did the book end up at Random House?

MALCOLM: There was a problem about publishing it at the
time the contract said it would be published, so I withdrew
the book. It's hard for me to get to work on one thing when
there's another thing still unpublished.

    But another good thing about the change was it permitted
me to write more. At Random House I was permitted and
encouraged to write more. I feel the book is more complete
now than it would have been.

GOLDBERG: You've spent a lot of time thinking and writing about biographies. In this book, you wrote, "Chekhov's privacy is safe from the biographer's attempts upon it—as, indeed, are all privacies, even those of the most apparently open and even exhibitionistic natures. The letters and journals we leave behind and the impressions we have made on our contemporaries are the mere husk of the kernel of our essential life. When we die, the kernel is buried with us. This is the horror and pity of death and the reason for the inescapable triviality of biography." So it's almost like you started out feeling that you cannot write an accurate biography, that it's not a possibility.

MALCOLM: Well, if you notice I haven't written a biography really, though there's some biographical stuff in there, even while I was kind of interrogating the whole question of biography—that's a sort of theme of mine.

GOLDBERG: Right. And yet you did attempt something like a biography anyway.

MALCOLM: I know. That's an inconsistency. But I was conscious of never going beyond what's factual, never trying to imagine what he thought. I don't think I did; I hope I didn't—you know, that kind of reading of the mind. I tried to stay as factual as possible.

GOLDBERG: In researching this book, you spent several weeks in Russia. But the very first scene of your book—sitting with your guide in Yalta where Anna and Gurov sat in "The Lady With the Dog"—reads like kind of a farce, as if you're sitting there not really expecting any insights and nothing is happening, and yet you're pretending to be thrilled. And it sounded to me, reading what you wrote, that you didn't go there expecting any revelations to occur, so I wondered why you went.

MALCOLM: You mean you feel I kind of tipped my own hand?

GOLDBERG: It seemed to me that you were setting out to do this with a sense of irony about it.

MALCOLM: I guess that's true, because the great experience is the reading of the story, so what could be there in that same place? And why would you get from that place what Chekhov got from it?

And yet somehow I felt that I needed to go to Russia. I felt a very strong pull to go there, even though I've been skeptical of going to the places where something was written and having an experience that is equivalent. I think people who think that way may be having a self-fulfilling prophecy. But anyway, I went, reluctantly. I don't like traveling very much. And then when I lost my suitcase, everything was awful.

GOLDBERG: But that was a great moment. You wrote: "When my suitcase was taken something else had been restored to me—*feeling itself* . . . Travel . . . is a low-key emotional experience, a pallid affair in comparison to ordinary life." And that realization gave you insight into "The Lady With the Dog," in which Anna, vacationing in Yalta, finds it "so dull here!"

MALCOLM: Also it was journalistically so fortunate. I mean, this is why one does it—because things happen and then you can write about them.

GOLDBERG: You often comment about people in your work that they "don't add up." You said in *The Journalist and the Murderer* about Joe McGinniss, "Like McGinniss' MacDonald, my McGinniss doesn't quite add up." You also said in *The Silent Woman* that Anne Stevenson's portrait of Sylvia Plath did not add up, and you said in your essay "The Trial of Alyosha" [in the collection *The Purloined Clinic*], "The Russian novelists knew in the most uncanny way how complicated we all are, how we don't add up." Can you talk about that?

MALCOLM: One of the answers to that is in Chekhov, in that same story, "The Lady With the Dog"—the passage about private life, you know? That we just don't make ourselves available:

> [He had two lives: one, open, seen and known by all who cared to know, full of relative truth and of relative falsehood, exactly like the lives of his friends and acquaintances; and another life running its course in secret. And through some strange, perhaps accidental, conjunction of circumstances, everything that was essential, of interest and of value to him, everything in which he was sincere and did not deceive himself, everything that made the kernel of his life, was hidden from

other people; and all that was false in him, the sheath in which he hid himself to conceal the truth—such, for instance, as his work in the bank, his discussions at the club, his "lower race," his presence with his wife at anniversary festivities—all that was open. And he judged of others by himself, not believing in what he saw, and always believing that every man had his real, most interesting life under the cover of secrecy and under the cover of night.]

That's the problem of biographers, is to get to the self.

The more I think about the problem of biography, the more I think you just have to be roughly right. I mean, there's kind of an agreement that one subject is more gentle and recessive and reticent, while another is aggressive and exhibitionistic. But what I am going through, inside myself, for instance, you'd never know.

GOLDBERG: Do we ourselves add up?

MALCOLM: No, of course we don't.

GOLDBERG: Given that, it's an impossible task to portray anybody.

MALCOLM: But I think people have an atmosphere, and you will write about me in some way that will say something about my atmosphere.

GOLDBERG: Do you think that you and what you write about were affected in some fundamental way by being sued by

Jeffrey Masson?

MALCOLM: Well, certainly *The Trial of Sheila McGough* [*sic*]; I probably would not have been interested in the law otherwise. That book, certainly, is very much related to my experiences in a lawsuit.

GOLDBERG: And *The Journalist and the Murderer*? I know you said in an afterword to the book that there wasn't any connection. But that seemed, I don't want to say disingenuous, but the connection I saw was that I imagined you sitting and taking notes and listening to Masson talk, and digging this grave for himself, making a fool of himself. And you were smiling and nodding and writing it all down, while you must have known you were going to basically eviscerate him. And that raised moral issues for you.

MALCOLM: There are two things I want to say. One is that when I wrote *The Journalist and the Murderer*, I thought my case was over, because the judge had dismissed it. If it hadn't been over I don't think I would have wanted to write that book.

The other point is that the real ideology of *The Journalist and the Murderer* came out of an intervening piece. I didn't write *The Journalist and the Murderer* right after the Masson lawsuit. I wrote a long piece about a woman named Ingrid Sischy ["A Girl of the Zeitgeist," 1986], and I interviewed her for over a year, and during those interviews we did a great deal of talking about this subject. Then I got that letter from McGinniss's lawyer and it kind of dovetailed. But then the book was unpopular. People were angry at the first sentence, at the lead, and then by that time the Masson case was being appealed.

GOLDBERG: It was a bad confluence.

MALCOLM: Yes, a bad confluence. [But the Sischy interviews were] where I became very conscious of it as a subject, rather than, as you were speculating, while I was interviewing Masson. That was not my view of what I was doing when I was interviewing Masson. I personally liked what I wrote. I mean, that's the way he was; I tape-recorded him and wrote about him as he was. And sometimes people don't like themselves the way they are. So it was a surprise to me.

GOLDBERG: Would you be surprised today?

MALCOLM: I think I now more understand that there's a gap between what people would like to have written about themselves and what they project themselves as.

GOLDBERG: However, when you wrote that first sentence of *The Journalist and the Murderer*, you must have known then that you were going to antagonize journalists.

MALCOLM: I had no idea.

GOLDBERG: Really?

MALCOLM: Absolutely none. I just thought it was a nice piece of rhetoric, and actually my husband, who is my editor, said,

"You shouldn't begin this way, you should begin with some piece of history"—something that was more conventional. And then my daughter read it and said, "Oh, what happened to that sentence? You should put it back." So, probably, if it had been the way my husband said . . .

GOLDBERG: Your life would be very different.

MALCOLM: Yes, [that sentence] would have been buried there somewhere, and nobody would have . . .

GOLDBERG: Maybe, but you know, you've done it in other places as well. You said about biographers, for example, "The biographer at work is like a professional burglar breaking into a house, rifling through certain drawers that he has good reason to think contain the jewelry and money, and triumphantly bearing his loot away. The voyeurism and busybodyism that impel writers and readers of biography alike are obscured by an apparatus of scholarship designed to give the enterprise an appearance of bank-like blandness and solidity." So, you know you're being provocative, right? I'm not saying you're being the slightest bit inaccurate, I'm just saying it's probably going to offend some of the people who are going to be reading it.

MALCOLM: I think until all this tension began with the Masson case, I was living in this kind of nice, protected environment, at *The New Yorker*. I knew the readers were somewhere out there, but I felt very private and I wrote for the people I knew. But after all this stuff I became more conscious of writing in a larger community, and it's not as pleasant to write in that kind of subconsciousness than it had been.

GOLDBERG: But you didn't tone it down?

MALCOLM: I guess not.

GOLDBERG: What are you working on now?

MALCOLM: I'm working on art, actually. I'm making collages. I'm going to be in a group show in January at the Lori Bookstein gallery, and I'm thrilled about it.

GOLDBERG: Is this your first show?

MALCOLM: My first show, yes. There are sixteen of my collages there. I've been working on them for the last few years.

GOLDBERG: Do you see any relationship between your collages and your writing?

MALCOLM: I think so. I like to think about my work as kind of collage-like. A friend who's a critic [Lee Siegel] is going to write the catalog for the show, and he says he thinks there's a connection, so I'll be interested to read what he writes.

THE BETRAYAL OF THE SUBJECT

INTERVIEW BY DAPHNE BEAL
THE BELIEVER
OCTOBER 1, 2004

"Every journalist who is not too stupid or too full of himself to notice what is going on knows that what he does is morally indefensible," Janet Malcolm writes at the opening of *The Journalist and the Murderer* in the kind of fierce statement that has earned her a reputation as an unswerving truth teller. Like many of Malcolm's other nonfiction works, this book, published in 1990, takes a specific event (a murderer suing a journalist) and unpacks it so extensively that the work illuminates a larger topic—in this case, the complex psychological dynamics at the heart of the art of journalism.

Malcolm, who has been publishing pieces that seamlessly combine essay and reportage in *The New Yorker* since the late seventies, has written eight books, spanning such topics as the politics and pitfalls of the field of psychoanalysis (*Psychoanalysis: The Impossible Profession* [1981]), the problem of biography seen through the lens of Sylvia Plath (*The Silent Woman* [1994]), and a meditation on the life and work of Chekhov (*Reading Chekhov* [2001]). Others include *In the Freud Archives* (1984) and *The Crime of Sheila McGough* (1999), as well as two collections of essays, *The Purloined Clinic* (1992) and *Diana and Nikon* (1980, expanded in 1997). What grabs and regrabs the reader in her writing is its deft commingling of sleuthing and contemplation. Reading Malcolm, one has the sensation of being in the presence of a mind constantly in action on several levels, mediating between external reality (one most often consisting of facts that are at odds with one another) and her own consciousness. With the exception of *The Purloined Clinic*, none of her books is much more than two hundred pages, but the rigor of her writing gives them the quality of murals painted by a miniaturist.

Malcolm can be unsparing in her portrayals of the people she comes across, but her extraordinary precision does not preclude compassion. Occasionally, Malcolm's subjects damn themselves, but more often they reveal the vanities, obsessions, and desires that we all share—if to a heightened degree.

Currently at work on a book about Gertrude Stein and Alice B. Toklas, Malcolm corresponded with me by email between March and June of this year.

DAPHNE BEAL: It's interesting that we're doing this interview by email, because one of the phrases that's long been in my head is your description from *The Silent Woman* of letters written today on computers as being "marmoreally cool and smooth," in contrast to letters from previous decades written on manual typewriters. Correspondence plays such a large role in almost all your books, not just the content and tone, but often the texture and feel of the letters' pages. Email seems to up that smoothness even further. Do you use it a lot yourself, or are "real" letters still a preferred form? How do you think email has affected the way people communicate by the written word?

JANET MALCOLM: When I wrote *The Silent Woman*, email

had not yet arrived—or was not yet in common use. I would not use the phrase "marmoreally cool and smooth" about email. I think of email as messy, both in appearance and in the character of the writing. Email encourages a kind of laxness, a letting down of hair. When I write a "real" letter, I care about how it looks. I will compulsively redo a letter if the indentations aren't uniform or if I've smudged the signature. With email, I don't know what the message will look like on the receiver's screen. I only know it will be surrounded by all kinds of stuff—titles, "headers," numbers, codes, etc.—that I had nothing to do with. So I take no trouble over the appearance of the message. I take some trouble over the message itself, but not as much as I would in a letter. Doing this interview by email gives me a chance to think of answers to your questions. If we did it in person, I might just look at you in blank helplessness.

BEAL: Reading your work, it's hard to ever imagine you with such a look! I'm always amazed by the quick turns, the dips and dives through any given moment of interaction, especially when it comes to the psychological underpinnings of things. I read somewhere that your father was a psychiatrist. Did that mean you were very aware of psychology as a philosophy/art/science from an early age? Was that a field you ever seriously considered going into?

MALCOLM: No, I never considered becoming a psychiatrist or psychoanalyst, and while growing up I paid little attention to my father's work. He himself was not all that invested in it—for many years he was head psychiatrist of an outpatient clinic of the Veterans Administration. He loved nature, literature, and sports, and he was a gifted comic writer. Unfortunately, he wrote in Czech, and Czech wit does not translate well. This is not to say that he didn't excel in his work as a psychiatrist (and as a neurologist, his second specialty). He just wasn't pompous about it—as many psychiatrists were in those days. He had affectionate regard for his patients and no use for social workers. He was wonderfully satiric about them and their clipboards. A piece of writing of mine that is connected to my father is "The One-Way Mirror," about the family therapist Salvador Minuchin. Would you like me to tell you about that?

BEAL: Sure, I'm a sucker for anything about families and their influence.

MALCOLM: In the late seventies I gave up smoking and, naturally, couldn't write. I decided to do what *The New Yorker* called a long fact piece, which would require many months of reporting. I figured that by the time I finished the reporting I would be ready to try writing without smoking. I remembered something my father had told me about a remarkable man who cured anorectic girls in one session—at lunch with their families, at the end of which the girls would eat, the way cripples would walk at the end of faith-healing encounters. He had seen this man perform at a hospital near his clinic, and marveled at his powerful personality. I had never heard my father speak so enthusiastically about anyone in psychiatry, and decided to make that man, Minuchin, the subject of my piece. For many months I took the train to Philadelphia where Minuchin had a clinic, and watched him instruct a class of young psychiatrists in his kind of theatrical family therapy. When it was time to write, I found I could write without smoking. This was the first long fact piece I had ever done, and this kind of writing turned out to be congenial to me.

BEAL: How many years into your writing career were you when that happened? And did that process of choosing Minuchin for your subject matter become in any way a prototype for how you've chosen other topics?

MALCOLM: When I wrote "The One-Way Mirror," I had been writing for about ten years. I had done book reviews, essays on photography, and pieces about decorative art. But I had never done reportage. The way I stumbled on Minuchin as a subject is pretty much the way I stumble on all my journalistic subjects. I hear or read about someone, or someone writes to me. My book *The Crime of Sheila McGough* came out of a letter I received from its heroine, who thought I might be interested in her story of going to prison for a crime she didn't commit. Journalists get a lot of letters like that, but this one had an unusual atmosphere (and wasn't on yellow lined paper), so I wrote back. But why am I telling you this? Because you asked. One of the things that journalists come to understand after doing journalism for a while is the power of the question.

BEAL: I want to come back to Sheila McGough, but at the moment I'll make a kind of left turn if that's okay. Last fall you had an exhibit of your collages at the Lori Bookstein gallery here in New York City, a medium (as I understand it) that you've been working in more privately for some time. How did you come to work in collage, and what kind of questions does the medium ask or answer that writing does not? Or is it more related to your writing than I'm supposing?

MALCOLM: To try to answer your question, let me quote from a piece I wrote about ten years ago about the artist David Salle: "Writers have traditionally come to painters' ateliers in search of aesthetic succor. To the writer, the painter is a fortunate alter ego, an embodiment of the sensuality and exteriority that he has abjured to pursue his invisible, odorless calling. The writer comes to the places where traces of making can actually be seen and smelled and touched expecting to be inspired and enabled, possibly even cured. While I was interviewing the artist David Salle, I was coincidentally writing a book that was giving me trouble, and although I cannot pin it down exactly (and would not want to), I know that after each talk with Salle in his studio something clarifying and bracing did filter down to my enterprise." Quoting this excerpt—apart from telling you something about my attitude toward artists—enacts what I do as a collagist. I have taken something from one place (the Salle piece) and put it into another (this interview). It also exemplifies what I do when I write. I do an enormous amount of quoting—of people and texts—in my books and articles. David Salle is a painter who does nothing but "quote" or "appropriate" in his paintings. But that is another subject. I guess what I have been trying to say is that, yes, collage is "more related to [my] writing than [you're] supposing."

BEAL: I remember reading about your showing your collages to Salle, but it seems like another thing altogether to show your work in a gallery. How, if at all, has exhibiting your work changed your relationship to it? For one thing, is it as fun?

MALCOLM: When I first started exhibiting I was ambivalent about the idea of people buying my collages. When you publish a book, the text remains in your possession, so to speak. When you sell a painting or drawing or collage, you lose it. It goes out of your life. At first, I wasn't ready to let go of my work. Now I am. I am happy when someone buys a collage. There are a lot of them now. I feel I can keep making them. But even as I say this, I feel a little stab of regret about the collages that are hanging on the walls of strangers, and that it is unlikely I will ever see again. As for whether the work is as enjoyable as it was before I began to exhibit, the answer is no. I work harder. My standard of craftsmanship is higher and so is my idea of what is good enough to show.

BEAL: It does seem that while your writing and collage share certain qualities, the truth that collage is after is much more open-ended than writing's. I'm thinking in particular of your eloquent (that is, jaw-dropping) opening of *The Journalist and the Murderer*, about the inevitable betrayal by the journalist of the subject in the name of a higher truth. The theme of betrayal is echoed in much of your writing—the biographer of the subject, the protégé of the mentor, the photographer of the subject (Diane Arbus especially comes to mind), Gertrude Stein of the Jews around her, etc. I wonder if you would comment on this recurring motif?

MALCOLM: I did not set out to write about betrayal, but by writing about journalism, biography, and photography I kept bumping into it. In each of these genres the practitioner has an enormous amount of power over the subject. Apart from the practitioner's use or misuse of this power, the genres themselves have a built-in tendency to be unkind. It isn't only Diane Arbus who betrays the subjects of her photographs. Most people who have their picture taken hate the result. And most people who are the subjects of newspaper or magazine stories feel at least a little wronged if not outright betrayed. As for the illustrious dead . . .

BEAL: Being so thoroughly engaged in one of those inherently unkind professions, how do you reconcile the "not-niceness" (to borrow your description of the *Ariel* poems) of the finished piece with the process of asking your subject for his or her trust? Does that person occupy a different place in your thinking by the time you've finished writing than he or she did when you were in the thick of interviewing?

MALCOLM: In answer to your first question: You do not reconcile it. That is the moral problem of journalism. But journalists don't ask for the subject's trust—they don't have to. Subjects just give it. They are eager to tell their story and don't seem to realize that they are not invisible as they tell it. Incidentally, the final product of the inherently unkind professions isn't always not-nice. There are photographs in which the subject looks beautiful, and there are biographies and journalistic portraits from which the subject emerges as a great soul. I recently had the pleasure and privilege of writing about Anton Chekhov, about whom it is simply impossible to find anything seriously bad to say. Some of his biographers have tried—and failed. I'm not sure I understand your second question. Could you put it more simply? (I'm reading Gertrude Stein's *The Making of Americans*, which may explain my difficulty in understanding a sentence that isn't simple and hasn't been repeated a hundred times.)

BEAL: I think what I'm really asking for is advice. In my own experience I find it incredibly difficult when writing about someone to transition from that human connection that happens in the most fruitful of interviews to the more critical stance I need to take afterward. Because Chekhov seems to be part of a very small minority of people, dead or alive, of whom one can say nothing bad, and because people's contradictions are among their most interesting qualities, the writer has to be able to step back from that intimate place of interviewing (or research)—where practically anyone's reality can seem like the truth for at least a moment—to a more objective point of view. This often feels like an almost painful betrayal to me. What I wanted to find out (in my thickly veiled previous question) was how do you make the switch from supplicant or equal interviewer to authority writer? Is this clearer? If not, we can just abandon this line of thinking. I also realize that *The Journalist and the Murderer* addresses this question in book-length form.

MALCOLM: I'm glad I asked. What you write is very eloquent. Yes, I wrote about this dilemma in *The Journalist and the Murderer*, but I did not exhaust the subject by any means.

You bring something new into the discussion with your comment about the journalist's momentary identification with the subject. Since you are a novelist, you probably have more capacity for this kind of imaginative leap. I am incapable of writing fiction, so I am probably less empathic. But this doesn't seem to make any difference to the subject. He or she assumes your empathy—and then feels betrayed when what you write isn't like something he or she dictated to you. I put it another way in *The Journalist and the Murderer* (if you'll forgive me for quoting from myself again): "The journalistic encounter seems to have the same regressive effect on a subject as the psychoanalytic encounter. The subject becomes a kind of child of the writer, regarding him as a permissive, all-accepting, all-forgiving mother, and expecting that the book will be written by her. Of course, the book is written by the strict, all-noticing, unforgiving father." But getting back to your anxiety about the discontinuity between the coziness of the interview and the coldness of the act of writing—yes, it is a problem and no, it can't be resolved. When you make the switch from "supplicant or equal interviewer to authority writer" you are, like every other journalist, committing some sort of moral misdemeanor.

BEAL: So maybe the adjustment I need to make is simply downgrading my transgression from felony to misdemeanor. I was thinking, too, about your reputation as a writer for being quite exacting towards, or even tough on, your subjects. The same rigor that thrills some of your readers seems to make others extremely uncomfortable. I wonder if you've ever felt that the reception to your work has been colored by the fact that you're a woman. Are women still meant to be "nicer" as writers, less difficult? I ask because I think of my own interviewing style, at least in person, as incorporating some stereotypical feminine behavior: slightly low status and deferential, punctuated by ready laughter, and driven by an accommodating attitude. Later, when I'm writing I feel I've acted as something of a wolf in sheep's clothing. I remember your description of your "more Japanese technique" in *The Journalist and the Murderer*, in contrast to the more flat-footed *Newsday* reporter's. I have a sense of course, but wondered specifically what you meant by that?

MALCOLM: I really don't know whether the people who don't like my writing don't like it because of their perception of me as a tough, not-nice woman. It seems kind of ridiculous—I think of myself as a completely ordinary harmless person—but what people think of your writing persona is out of your hands. The narrator of my nonfiction pieces is not the same person I am—she is a lot more articulate and thinks of much cleverer things to say than I usually do. I can imagine her coming across as a little insufferable sometimes. But she, too, is out of my hands—I may have invented her, but she is the person who insists on speaking for me. As for the wolf in sheep's clothing question, perhaps the way to minimize one's feeling that one has not been as straightforward with the subject as one should have been, is to be a little more straightforward. To swallow the too-nice thing one is about to say. To remember that the subject is going to say what he or she wants to say no matter what you say or don't say. You can't keep your mouth shut all the time, of course, but you do well to keep it shut a lot of the time. If silence falls, let the subject break it—even though that's a very hard thing to do. By the way, I don't think the "feminine behavior" you describe is limited to women journalists. Men journalists can be just as ingratiating, deferential, accommodating, and laughter prone. When you ask what I mean by the Japanese technique, you are not employing it.

BEAL: Your answer really made me chuckle. I can't say exactly why except I think it has to do with the endless conundrum of writing—the fact that it seems so much in one's control (especially in contrast to, say, theater or visual art), and yet still there is that mystery of who is this character who insists on speaking for me? The undeniable fact that in the end the work and its effect are out of one's hands. Maybe then this is a good time to turn to the simultaneously charming and irascible Stein—speaking of being difficult. (I remember during my Midwestern childhood in the seventies confusing Gertrude Stein and Gloria Steinem, because, well, they were both considered impossible by local standards, but that's another story . . .) How did you come to write about her and Toklas? Is that *New Yorker* piece being turned into a book, and have you finished it?

MALCOLM: You made me chuckle too with your wonderful mixing up of Gertrude and Gloria. Yes, I am continuing to write about Stein. No, I have not finished. It is an exceptionally beautiful day today, and I am reminded of what Stein wrote (or said she wrote) on an exam paper in a course at Radcliffe given by William James: "Dear Professor James, I am so sorry but really I do not feel a bit like an examination paper in philosophy today." James (according to Stein) sent her a postcard saying: "Dear Miss Stein, I understand perfectly how you feel. I often feel like that myself," and gave her the highest grade in the class. There is reason to think that this didn't happen the way Stein said it did. But anyway, may I be excused from the examination today?

BEAL: Dear Miss Malcolm, I understand perfectly how you feel. I often feel like that myself. [And a week later . . .] Your response to the GS question left me unsure of whether you'd rather not talk about her at all right now, but my Malcolm-fan friends have been pressing me to ask why her, why now? I wondered if Stein's larger-than-life personality and work drew you initially to write about her, or if it was the question of her being Jewish and staying in France that began your investigation? In contrast to Chekhov, she seems to be a more problematic literary figure and her writing arguably less universally loved than his. It made me wonder if the topic of your last book pushed you in a different direction for the next. Or, conversely, I was thinking about the continuity—if there is more pleasure in writing about the "illustrious dead" than living subjects at the moment?

MALCOLM: I told you earlier how I stumble on subjects for pieces. I stumbled on the Gertrude Stein-in-wartime piece when *The New Yorker* asked me to contribute to an issue on food. I decided to write about *The Alice B. Toklas Cook Book.* While rereading Toklas's chapter on what she cooked during the German occupation of France, I became curious about

Stein and Toklas's wartime history. The longer piece followed my short piece about trying to cook a weird dish involving artichoke hearts and asparagus and calf brains. (The asparagus spears were somehow supposed to stand erect in a mush of calf brains and béchamel sauce.) I'm planning to write more about Stein and Toklas, but I can't really say why right now. I may know when I've written the piece. As for whether it's more agreeable to write about the illustrious dead than about the living, I'd say it all depends on which dead and which living.

BEAL: I laughed again, mostly because I was afraid of what would happen if I thought too much about the idea of "a mush of calf brains." Re: dead v. living subjects, how did the prolonged Masson suit affect your choice of subjects after that, if at all? I don't mean to belabor this question of choosing subject matter, but again I've been reflecting on how one knows what will make a good topic over a lengthy period of time—satisfying both the need for a certain meatiness and challenge, and for a pleasure in the task.

MALCOLM: Until this moment you were the first interviewer who did not bring Jeffrey Masson into the discussion. I guess that isn't possible after all. What you seem to be asking is whether being sued by him has made me leery of writing about people who are alive rather than safely dead. The answer is no. One of the reasons I refused to settle the Masson lawsuit (as the people he previously sued, Muriel Gardiner and Kurt Eissler, had done) was to leave no doubt in the minds of readers and future subjects that Masson's accusations of misquotation were untrue. As it turned out, a year after he lost his lawsuit at trial, my two-year-old granddaughter pulled a red notebook out of a bookcase, in which the things Masson said he didn't say were scribbled in my hand. The notes had been lost for ten years. The jury had decided to believe me anyway. But if the notebook hadn't got misplaced, there would have been no lawsuit. Your reflections on your desire to find a subject that is meaty and challenging and pleasurable to write about interest me very much. They remind me of one experience I had of not taking pleasure in a subject. That was the subject—business crime—of my book *The Crime of Sheila McGough*. To master the intricacies of the con of a certain con man was very difficult for me. I may not have solved the problem of how not to bore the reader with what gave me enormous trouble to understand. The book was not popular. But I have a special fondness for it, though I may be wrong about its merits.

BEAL: Sorry to be so tiresome as to bring up Masson, just like the rest. I think it's impossible not to because it does sound like it was such an ordeal, and when I think about events or circumstances in my own life that affect my writing, it's hard not to be curious. My final question is a two-parter. First of all, I was intrigued by what you wrote about the Sheila McGough book, about your special fondness for it, and I wondered if you would say a bit more. It sounds like it gave you some trouble in the writing. Is that difficulty where the fondness springs from? (Sometimes I think I may have assigned too much value to pleasurability in the writing process . . .) The second part is one of my reprise questions, and it has to do with email (just to complete the circle). In the course of our interview, I've often thought about your description of email as a letting down of one's hair and inherently messy, and tried to figure out if I agree. Messy, yes, but is it truly a letting down of one's hair, especially when the person on the other end isn't particularly known? I've often felt that email has a kind of conscious messiness (as in, "Well, this isn't perfectly articulated, but hopefully she'll know what I mean . . ."), whereas talk seems like the messiest form of communication of all, the way things slip out. In short, my question is this, at the end of this interview, has your opinion of email changed any since your original answer, and is this the first interview you've done by email?

MALCOLM: To answer the first part of your question, about why I am specially fond of *The Crime of Sheila McGough*: I like its oddness. I think it may be the most original of my books. I like the second part where I travel to the South to interview various strange persons, and the coda where I go to Treasure Mountain, where Bob Bailes, the con man, was going to build a fantastic resort, and where I find a peaceful late summer landscape. I like the book's own late summer melancholy. And, of course, I like Sheila McGough, a most unusual and sad person. Finally, I was glad to use some of what being a defendant myself taught me about the law and lawyers. Without that knowledge, I would not have been able to write (or even been interested in writing) the book. About email. Yes, this is my first email interview, and yes, talk is the messiest medium of all. Any transcript of a tape recording confirms that. Email lies somewhere between speech and proper writing. But I don't consider our interview a true example of email. Knowing that what I write will be published, I naturally take some trouble over it, and I assume you have done the same. So, no my opinion of email hasn't changed because I haven't really availed myself here of its permission to write sloppily.

After reading the interview, Malcolm sent the following in an email.

MALCOLM: I read the interview in the way one looks at photographs of oneself, and, except for one place, I thought I came out looking okay. But the exception may be the most interesting part of the interview. I'm talking about the place where you ask me about the Masson lawsuit. Until that moment the atmosphere of the interview is friendly and collegial, almost conspiratorial. Now it turns icy. I make an unpleasant observation and then launch into an absurd defense of myself. In defense of my defensiveness, I can only say that for a long time I wrongly assumed everyone would know that the accusations against me weren't true. Now, having finally learned that accusations must be answered at once, I ridiculously answer accusations that, years later, no one is making. But what is most interesting about this moment in our interview is the illustration it offers of a subject's feeling of betrayal when he or she realizes that the journalist is writing his or her own story. In my version of the story of my writing life, I wouldn't give Masson any role whatever. But your version—and any other good journalist's—would naturally give him a role. The lawsuit happened and my wish to deny its significance cannot cut any ice with you. My getting all huffy about your natural and not at all badly intentioned question just goes to show that even journalists are not immune to the vanity and self-deception that interviews bring out in their subjects and that journalists, like novelists, lie in wait for.

FROM GERTRUDE STEIN TO TRUE CRIME

INTERVIEW BY ELEANOR WACHTEL
WRITERS AND COMPANY
2008

ELEANOR WACHTEL: What first made you want to write about these two lives of Gertrude Stein and Alice B. Toklas?

JANET MALCOLM: It started this way. I was asked to contribute to an issue of the *New Yorker*. The subject was food, and I thought I would write about *The Alice B. Toklas Cookbook*. And I did write a short piece, cooking some of the recipes. As I was reading the cookbook, I came to a chapter that did not have the gravy stains that the other chapters did. It was about the wartime cooking that Alice and Gertrude had done. Alice had actually done the cooking and Gertrude just did the eating. And I began to wonder . . . They lived in Vichy, France, throughout the war. I wondered how these Jewish lesbians had survived under the Nazis. I started doing some research on that. And that's how the book began.

WACHTEL: Although your book was about two lives, it was Gertrude Stein who claimed the spotlight. She was born in 1874, the youngest of five children. What do we know about her family?

MALCOLM: She came from a Jewish immigrant family. She was raised in Oakland, California. Her mother died when she was young—she was a young teenager—died of cancer. And she followed her brother Leo, who was at Harvard, and studied at Radcliffe.

WACHTEL: Stein was especially close to her brother Leo, who was about two years older, and initially lived with him in Paris after Radcliffe. What was it about their relationship that worked so well?

MALCOLM: Their relationship worked very well when they were children, and they were the two smartest kids and the two closest in age. It worked very well at Harvard/Radcliffe and afterward in Baltimore, when she was in medical school and he was doing some kind of research. But it stopped working when she began writing. He didn't like her writing and felt that he was—as he called it—the genius. That was a struggle: Who is the genius of the family? And then they fell apart, stopped living together, and stopped ever seeing each other.

WACHTEL: That seems extreme.

MALCOLM: Very extreme, yes. But Gertrude Stein didn't do things by halves.

WACHTEL: There's a wonderful illustration of her supreme self-confidence. I'm thinking of an exam that she was supposed to sit for a philosophy course at Radcliffe taught by William James in the late 1890s. Can you describe what happened?

MALCOLM: She had gone to the opera the night before and hadn't studied. So when she came into the examination room, she wrote into the exam book, "Dear Professor James, it's a beautiful day and I just don't feel like an examination," gave him the exam book, and left. Then the next day she got a postcard from William James saying, "Dear Miss Stein, I know exactly how you feel"—and he gave her an A, of course.

WACHTEL: It's astounding. Where did this self-assuredness come from?

MALCOLM: It's a complicated question, because we don't really know. We can only speculate. And some of the self-assurance could have come from its opposite—that she wasn't so self-assured as she sounded. But I think her status as a youngest child did a lot to give her this feeling that things were going to go right for her in the world.

WACHTEL: You say that her whole life was like that?

MALCOLM: Well, as she wrote about it in *The Autobiography of Alice B. Toklas*, which, as we all know, is her own autobiography, written in the voice of Alice, her companion.

WACHTEL: She wrote about how things go her way?

MALCOLM: Yes.

WACHTEL: You give an example about Picasso trying to paint her portrait, going through eighty or ninety sittings, and then giving up. And then suddenly, he just does it. Can you remember other instances in which her life turned out so fortunate?

MALCOLM: Again, this is her account, and she wrote *The Autobiography of Alice B. Toklas* as a sort of fairy tale of her coming to Paris and becoming part of the new art movement: buying the work of these great painters when they were still unknown—Picasso and Matisse. But another illustration occurred in World War I. She talks about seeing some lady who was an American helping the cause of the good guys in World War I. Gertrude said she wanted to help and the lady said, "Well you need to have a car if you want to help." So Gertrude wrote to somebody in America who very quickly sent her over a car so that she could help in World War I. So it's that kind of ease. It probably wasn't quite as easy as she made it out to be, but her life seemed to proceed along the lines she wanted it to proceed along.

WACHTEL: Despite some earlier insecurities, Stein did have a big ego and she seems to have had great charm as well, and people were attracted to her. How did that charm come across?

MALCOLM: People who knew her say she was just the most delightful, wonderful, warm person. A lot of them talked about her laugh—that she had some kind of a wonderful laugh. She just seemed to be one of these beguiling people. Some of this comes across a little bit in her experimental writing. You don't quite know what's going on in the writing but you feel a tremendous cheerfulness and energy, and self-confidence. That's the closest we can get to what she was like in life.

WACHTEL: You call that "pretty irresistible"—what's your own reaction to Stein?

MALCOLM: I can resist her [*laughs*], but as I worked on my book I came to grudgingly admire her. What seems very extraordinary about her is this very extreme passion for life that she had. I feel she lived in a fuller and more vital and maybe even more enjoyable way than most people do and this attracted me to her.

WACHTEL: Why grudging?

MALCOLM: Because the writing is so difficult. I came to Stein as many people do, just kind of resenting that she writes such difficult poetry and prose and makes no effort to be comprehensible. As a writer who tries to make sense myself, maybe that's part of this resentment that I may have more of than other readers.

WACHTEL: Do you think Gertrude Stein had a sense of humor about herself? A self-awareness?

MALCOLM: I think so, I do think so. She was very, very intelligent and she knew exactly what was going on.

WACHTEL: You were saying Gertrude Stein didn't do things by half. Most of Stein's friendships did end in quarreling and breakup. Was there a less charming side as well, or was this the sort of obverse of the charm?

MALCOLM: I would not agree with you that it was most, but there were many. Some friendships did last from beginning to end—like Carl van Vechten. This is probably getting ahead of our story, but there was that bad guy, the [*inaudible*] collaborator, and Thornton Wilder was a very good, dear friend. It's said that the friendships that didn't last didn't last because of Alice Toklas's intervention, that she became jealous of these friendships and did what she felt needed to be done so that Gertrude wouldn't go on being friends with them. Probably the most famous example of this is the friendship with Ernest Hemingway that started out wonderfully and then ended.

WACHTEL: Because Toklas subverted it?

MALCOLM: That seems to be the theory, and there may even be some evidence for it in correspondence.

WACHTEL: And also with an American, Mabel Dodge. She seemed jealous of her as well.

MALCOLM: Absolutely. There was that scene about the luncheon where some kind of an electric look passed between Mabel Dodge and Gertrude Stein, and Alice got up from the table—she just couldn't stand it—and never came back to the lunch. Then somehow that was the end. Mabel Dodge reports on that in one of her memoirs.

WACHTEL: That was the end of Mabel Dodge [*laughs*] in terms of a friendship [with Stein]. Janet Malcolm, Gertrude Stein's lifelong partner and most devoted protector was Alice B. Toklas. How do you think her character and personality fit in or around Stein?

MALCOLM: She played the role of the protector, the person who made her comfortable. The time when they were together was not a time when lesbians were out. So they kept that hidden. Alice Toklas was presented as her secretary and her companion—she did the cooking. And she was different from Alice in the most obvious ways: Gertrude Stein was fat; Alice was thin. Gertrude Stein was very exuberant; Alice was closed and discreet. Gertrude Stein was the naughty child wanting to have fun and Alice was a strict governess keeping her in line.

WACHTEL: Although Stein was the genius and Toklas the handmaiden, what was the real dynamic of the relationship?

MALCOLM: Biography really can't establish very much about interior life, but what we can surmise about their dynamic is that there was a lot of tension—and maybe even some of this kind of sadomasochism that Hemingway documented in one of his books.

WACHTEL: There's an incident concerning a manuscript of Stein's long poem—"Stanzas in Meditation"—where every instance of the word *may* is crossed out and replaced. Can you tell me about that?

MALCOLM: This was the discovery of Ulla Dydo, who is one of three scholars with whom I would meet while writing my book. We would talk about Stein and about their research. Ulla has done some of the deepest research on Stein and her task, as she saw it, was to establish a correct text of Stein's work. Stein wrote in this rather difficult handwriting, and Ulla sat for twenty years in the Yale library and compared the published to the handwritten texts, and found enormous numbers of mistakes. In the course of this work, she found this manuscript, a poem called "Stanzas in Meditation," and saw these "may's" crossed out and "can's" put in—the published versions all used "can." And she just couldn't figure it out—

WACHTEL: The "can's" made it even worse.

MALCOLM: It was very difficult to make out, but it made a little bit more sense when it was "may." When it was "can," it was hopeless. And Ulla Dydo had a dream which gave her the answer to her question of why this happened. To understand her dream, I'm going to tell a little history here. When Gertrude Stein was in medical school, she had a love affair with a woman named May Bookstaver. We don't know how far this affair went but she was madly in love with May Bookstaver, a young woman of her age. This ended badly, as young love affairs do. Going forward twenty, thirty years, one day Gertrude Stein was rifling through a closet with some literary friends and Alice was around, and came across the manuscript of a novel she had written about this love affair. Alice had not known about the novel and was deeply hurt that

Stein had never told her about the love affair. She was so angry about this that when she then read the poem, every time there was the word "may," because of May Bookstaver—as it was reconstructed by Ulla and her fellow scholars—she was standing over her and making her change every "may" to a "can."

WACHTEL: Why do you think Stein agreed to that?

MALCOLM: I guess because she was afraid of her. There was some kind of dynamic of that kind between them. So this gives us some kind of a clue that there was something very violent going on between them sometimes.

WACHTEL: Janet Malcolm, one of Stein's most significant works, if not the most read, is *The Making of Americans*. I like the way you talk about how you got yourself to tackle it.

MALCOLM: The one book in print now has very small, dense type. It's this very thick paperback, and I found it very hard to even lift, and I had it, but I didn't want to read it. I solved this problem by taking a kitchen knife and cutting it into six pieces, and then I could read it piece by piece, and carry it around with me, and read it on the subway. And I read it, as not many people have done.

WACHTEL: What was your reaction to it?

MALCOLM: Fascination. I was really fascinated with the form this book took. It's a book about Stein's struggle to become a writer and to understand people and to come to terms with grief and loss. It's a very strange, quite wonderful, and quite terrible book. So that was an interesting experience for me, to read this book, and I don't think I would have read it if I wasn't writing about it. I've done readings where I've read my chapter about this book, and I ask the audience if there's anyone who's read the book and, to date, nobody has.

WACHTEL: The characters in *The Making of Americans* aren't fleshed out. The narrator, as you point out, is the only person that the reader sees in any complexity. Stein herself seemed to be aware of this. Did that bother her, that she was the only real character in the book?

MALCOLM: It did bother her! She kept saying, "I'm so frustrated. I'm trying to write about people, but I can't." In a way, what the book is about is that she's not able to write fiction. She doesn't really know how to imagine people well enough. She kept struggling with this incapacity.

WACHTEL: She acknowledges that people are essentially unknowable, as we all might, but it's certainly a slow process. Do you think she lacked psychological acuity?

MALCOLM: I guess yes and no. She's very sharp, and I think part of the reason people liked her so much was because she understood interacting with people, so on that level she was a wonderful psychologist. But I think she didn't really know how to write about people. And this is what she's struggling with in this massive, strange book. And once she finished it, she never felt like she had to do anything like that again. She wrote poetry and these strange, wonderful, experimental works like her book *Tender Buttons*, which is about objects, and she became this really interesting avant-garde writer.

WACHTEL: It took her eight years to write *The Making of Americans*. How did that free her for later writing?

MALCOLM: It freed her by getting a lot of misery out of her system. It's almost as if she had to vomit to get this book out of herself. And it was out, and then she could be light and strange, and stop trying to do conventional fiction, and somehow she could become original.

WACHTEL: At the heart of *Two Lives* is your own question about Gertrude Stein and Alice B. Toklas during the Second World War. They were Jewish lesbians living freely in relative comfort in rural France during the Nazi occupation, which certainly raises some questions. First, why do you think they didn't go to Switzerland or back to America under the circumstances?

MALCOLM: Gertrude Stein wrote an article about this question. They were seriously thinking of going back to America and were cautioned by the embassy in Léon to go back. But then Gertrude said in a characteristic, cheerful way, "We're comfortable here, we like the food here, and it would be too difficult to move, so we're going to stay." Something like that. I'm sure hidden beneath that were lots of other anxieties and questions, but she tossed it off as a decision having to do with comfort.

WACHTEL: Do you think it was political naivete or do you think it went back to her longstanding belief that people would always help her?

MALCOLM: I think those are both elements of that strange decision. And of course their gamble did pay off.

WACHTEL: As so many others' didn't. People with money and privilege and everything.

MALCOLM: And her decision was like the decision of so many Jews across Europe. Nobody could imagine the catastrophe. Nobody knew what was coming, or could believe it. If you told anybody what was going to happen they'd think, "This is some kind of horrible fantasy." So I don't think she behaved so strangely, given what was not known.

WACHTEL: Maybe the strange part is that the gamble paid off. And that was because, as always, someone did come to Stein's aid. This time it was Bernard Faÿ, who was an old friend. Tell me about him.

MALCOLM: He was a friend of Stein and Toklas from the '20s, I think. They met him at one of the parties they went to. He was a history professor, very intelligent, belonged to a Catholic royalist family, and he and Gertrude Stein became very very good friends. He translated some of her work into French. And then when the Nazis took over he became a collaborator. I don't think they knew—I'm sure they didn't know the extent of his collaboration, which was very deep, and bad. But he had ties to Petain and he protected them. And it's believed that this is why they survived, because they had his protection.

WACHTEL: By all accounts, even apart from his later collaboration with the Nazis, Faÿ doesn't seem to be very likeable. What do you think his friendship with Stein and Toklas was based on?

MALCOLM: I think he was very likeable to them, especially to Gertrude—

WACHTEL: —because he was an admirer.

MALCOLM: —because he was an admirer, a very good flatterer. He had a very good oily, flattering manner. And he was also smart, it wasn't only flattery, there was something that he gave to Gertrude Stein. He apparently wrote some good books about American history. He was in this country, he taught here, at some point. When Gertrude Stein, after *The Autobiography of Alice B. Toklas*, did a speaking tour in America, he helped her. He facilitated many of the lectures he gave. He even coached her on lecturing. He was a very nice part of her life even though he was not a nice man by all other accounts.

WACHTEL: And he was anti-Semitic, so why would he befriend two Jewish women?

MALCOLM: I puzzle about that and talk about this "some

of my best friends are Jews" thing. It's known that many anti-Semites do have a "pet Jew" that they have a strong relationship with.

WACHTEL: The war drew attention to the fact that Stein and Toklas didn't acknowledge their Jewishness. What do you think this passive refusal was about?

MALCOLM: I think it had to do with the spirit of the time, when there was still a lot of anti-Semitism everywhere. They were not the only Jews who were quiet about being Jewish. It's a problem for many readers of the book, who have been very critical of them and of their war. I'm not critical of them because I feel that, who are we to say what we would have done in the same situation. They didn't do anything bad. Bernard Faÿ did really bad things. He was obsessed with freemasons, and he was the cause of the imprisonment and death of many freemasons and also some Jews. They survived, they did no harm to anybody. They didn't do anything heroic, but they didn't do anything bad. So I feel I can't be critical of them.

WACHTEL: At the end of wars, I have seen, Gertrude Stein alludes to what happens to others.

MALCOLM: As if it was then that she first learned about the camps and about the persecution of the Jews. I don't think she knew nothing, she obviously knew something. Already Jews were being rounded up in Paris and all over France, so she knew something, but probably not as much as she learned later.

WACHTEL: You've looked into the biographical enterprise before, especially in your work *The Silent Woman*, which focuses on the biographers of Sylvia Plath, and their battles or encounters with the Plath estate: at the time, Plath's husband, Ted Hughes, and his sister Olwyn. What drew you to their story?

MALCOLM: Like my beginnings with Stein and Toklas, it just kind of came out of left field. I happened to have gone to the University of Michigan with Anne Stevenson, who had written a biography of Sylvia Plath which was greatly criticized for being too friendly to Ted Hughes. I started looking into this, just as I started looking into Gertrude and Alice's war because of the cookbook, and one thing led to another.

WACHTEL: You describe how you got involved in a curious way. I wonder if you could just read a paragraph or so from *The Silent Woman*.

MALCOLM: "In a letter that appeared in the *New York Review of Books*, September 30th, 1976, written in response to a review of three books about Plath, Olwyn Hughes complains that the reviewer Karl Miller treats Sylvia Plath's family as if they are characters in some work of fiction. She says further, 'It is almost as though writing about Sylvia, some of whose work seems to take cruel and poetically licensed aim at those nearest to her, journalists feel free to do the same.' Of course they do. The freedom to be cruel is one of journalism's uncontested privileges, and the rendering of subjects as if they were characters in bad novels is one of its widely accepted conventions. In Mrs. Plath, Ted Hughes, and Olwyn Hughes, journalism found, and continues to find, three exceptionally alluring targets for its sadism and reductionism. When *Bitter Fame* appeared and raised the stakes of the game (*Bitter Fame* is the Anne Stevenson book), I decided to become a player. Like all the other players at the table, I felt anxious and oppressed by the game. It is being played in a room so dark and gloomy that one has a hard time seeing one's hand. One is apt to make mistakes. The air in the room is bad. It is the same air that has been breathed there for many years. The windows are grimy and jammed shut. The old servant's hands shake as he brings watery drinks. Through a door, one sees an open coffin surrounded by candles. A small old woman sits in a straight-backed chair reading a manual of stenography. A very tall man with graying hair in black comes through the doorway, having to duck his head, and stands watching the players. The door to the street suddenly opens, and a tall woman bursts in. she whispers something into the tall man's ear. He shrugs and returns to the room with the coffin. She looks after him, then gives the card table a malevolent little shove, so the drinks spill and cards scatter, and leaves, slamming the door. I look at my cards, and call the bet."

WACHTEL: Janet Malcolm, reading from her book *The Silent Woman*. Why a card game? Why call the bet? The whole metaphor is quite striking, and it's not like anything else in your book, which is a more straightforward account.

MALCOLM: I know, reading it now it does seem very strange to me! [*Laughs*] I don't know where it came from. Sometimes the unconscious comes out when you least expect it and reading this really surprised me—it was a very interesting experience. It's very strange and I have no idea where it comes from.

WACHTEL: It's almost like a haunting.

MALCOLM: Yes!

WACHTEL: Two of the main difficulties that Anne Stevenson had to contend with when she was writing *Bitter Fame* were Ted Hughes and his sister Olwyn Hughes, who managed Plath's estate at the time. You met and corresponded with Olwyn, what was she like?

MALCOLM: She was quite magnificent. She was very fierce, she was very mad at a lot of people.

WACHTEL: She's the tall woman? Entering and whispering in the dark man's ear and storming out.

MALCOLM: I guess she must be the tall woman. I guess I must have had her in mind. And I guess Ted was the tall man, the man in black. And Sylvia's in the coffin . . . I'm really quite amazed by that piece of writing, very atypical. I liked Olwyn a lot. She was so pure in her dislike of the people she thought were harming her brother, and she was very protective of Ted. She was like one of these dogs that growls if you come too close to its master and doesn't seem to have good intentions. I never met Ted Hughes. I corresponded with him through his publisher, and the reason I corresponded was because I wanted to be able to quote from some of his wonderful letters, and I needed the permission.

WACHTEL: Were you disappointed you didn't get to meet him?

MALCOLM: I didn't try to meet him while writing the book. I wanted him to be an absent figure. I wanted his voice to be there through his writings. And he was very generous about the book after it came out. He said he liked it and we had a nice correspondence. I thought I would one day meet him—I was very, very sad when he died. I knew I never would.

WACHTEL: Anne Stevenson had agreed to a close collaboration with Olwyn. Ted Hughes remained somewhat elusive or was only accessible to her through Olwyn, and this was when Stevenson was writing her biography of Sylvia Plath. But you describe that as entering a spider's web. What was the agreement about? Why would Anne Stevenson agree to it?

MALCOLM: I think it's always dangerous when you're writing to make any kind of deal with somebody else and to lose control of what you're doing. Anne Stevenson did seem to have ceded some control to Olwyn and it got very difficult for her to be writing her book with Olwyn at her shoulder telling her what to write. She did write her own book but it was very difficult.

WACHTEL: And she got criticized a lot, I mean the book was criticized.

MALCOLM: The book was criticized because it was thought that she was just expressing the party line about Hughes against Plath and many of the feminist admirers of Plath were very angry.

WACHTEL: Partway through *The Silent Woman*, you state your bias clearly: you're on the side of Ted Hughes. What was that based on? And does that necessarily bias you against Sylvia Plath? It seems this is an instance where everybody has to take sides—is that your sense?

MALCOLM: We all tend to take sides, and I felt that this pose of neutrality was wrong and I wanted to illustrate it with my own statement of a bias and put it right out there, rather than pretending to be writing something neutral, and that I was omniscient. I presented myself as a biased observer, like everybody else.

WACHTEL: Why were you on his side?

MALCOLM: I was on his side, not against Sylvia, not in relation to their relationship, but in relation to the abuse that had been heaped on him, and in the way his privacy had been invaded. He tried to live a life of his own and was constantly being plagued by the Sylvia Plath legend. It was very tragic what had happened to her and then what had happened to him. He wanted to be left alone and he wasn't, and I sympathize with that.

WACHTEL: Sylvia Plath killed herself at the age of 30. You give a glimpse of two sides of Plath that were at odds with each other. Not just any mental unbalance or suicidal inclinations, but I think that aspect of the 50s: that Plath both wanted a husband but also was quite fierce about her own writing and her desire to be a writer in her own right.

MALCOLM: But, until the end, her marriage was very fruitful for her poetry. Here she was married to a wonderful poet. When they first got together he was clearly the more advanced poet, she became the poet that she became over the period of the marriage, and those great *Ariel* poems were late. When she first met Hughes she was writing much weaker poetry, so it wasn't a question of her writing versus her marriage. It was a productive marriage as far as the work went. They helped each other. They were very nicely entwined as far as their work went. She was very helpful to him in getting his stuff published. He was not as aggressive as she was about getting this stuff out. She had received seventy rejections before her first story was published, and her mother would type things for her and help her get them out there. I think she took over that role with Hughes. And for his part, he was very supportive of her work, and very interested in her work. When she wrote those *Ariel* poems, which are very bitter about him and about men—there's that famous poem about "every woman loves a Fascist" and "daddy" and "the brute"—that came after he abandoned her for another woman. A lot of it was about that.

WACHTEL: The motives of your subjects are clearly of interest to you, and you've written books and journalism on psychoanalysis. What attracted you to that in the first place?

MALCOLM: I was in analysis myself, so then when I ended my analysis I was very curious about what had gone on. I wanted to know more about it, and I wanted to know what had been going on on the other side of the couch. I started interviewing analysts, and found this one analyst who had much more to say than the others did, and that was the man I called Aaron Green in my book *The Impossible Profession*.

WACHTEL: How would you say that being in analysis affected your writing or how you deal with subjects?

MALCOLM: One of the things that Aaron Green said that I think was very wise in that book is that the best you can hope for in analysis is change of a very tiny sort. If there is some little tiny change the analysis has succeeded. It's not a dramatic process at all. I would extend that to my writing. Probably there is something that is different being post-analysis, but nothing extreme.

WACHTEL: Is that enough, a little tiny change? Because you approach psychiatry with the same skepticism you bring to all your subjects, you observe that the crowning paradox of psychoanalysis is the near-uselessness of its insight. It's just a teeny tiny change, and was that enough for you?

MALCOLM: I think so. You've reminded me that I wrote a metaphor about this, which is water coming through a mesh and then the drops that remain on the mesh are what you've gotten, what you're left with. That small difference.

WACHTEL: Janet Malcolm, most of your work looks not only at the ostensible subject—Stein and Toklas, or Ted and Ol-wyn Hughes and Sylvia Plath—but the relationship between journalist or biographer and the subject. I wonder if you could read the opening from your book, *The Journalist and the Murderer*. The famous [opening]! You're laughing because it's become too famous, or it's haunted you?

MALCOLM: Something like that. In my family it was called the Gettysburg Address [*laughs*].

> Every journalist who is not too stupid or too full of him-self to know what is going on knows what he does is morally indefensible. He is a kind of confidence man, preying on people's vanity, ignorance, or loneliness, gaining their trust and betraying them without remorse. Like the credulous widow who wakes up one day to find the charming young man and all her savings gone, so the consenting subject of a piece of nonfiction writing learns—when the article or book appears—*his* hard les-son. Journalists justify their treachery in various ways according to their temperaments. The more pompous talk about freedom of speech and "the public's right to know"; the least talented talk about Art; the seemliest murmur about earning a living.
>
> The catastrophe suffered by the subject is no simple mat-ter of an unflattering likeness or a misrepresentation of his views; what pains him, what rankles and sometimes drives him to extremes of vengefulness, is the deception that has been practiced on him. On reading the article

or book in question, he has to face the fact that the journalist—who seemed so friendly and sympathetic, so
keen to understand him fully, so remarkably attuned to
his vision of things—never had the slightest intention of
collaborating with him on his story but always intended
to write a story of his own.

WACHTEL: Janet Malcolm, reading from the opening of *The
Journalist and the Murderer*. What makes people want to talk
and reveal themselves to the journalist or the biographer?

MALCOLM: Not everybody has this desire, but the people
who do feel they have a story to tell. They want to get that
story told, and they're not writers themselves. So the writer
becomes an instrument or vehicle for getting this story told. I
think that's the impulse.

WACHTEL: The idea of betrayal comes up frequently in your
work. There's an instance of a Gertrude Stein biographer, Leon
Katz, who's fearful of being betrayed, or the other biographers
who feel betrayed because he won't share his material. The feeling of betrayal to the biographers of Sylvia Plath. You've even
suggested that an autobiographer can set himself up for a betrayal no less profound than the subject of another's writing.
Why do you think the subject of betrayal is something that's
your subject?

MALCOLM: [*laughs*] That's very interesting. You're kind of
putting me on the spot.

WACHTEL: It's an intriguing subject because it involves conflict, which is inherently dramatic, and seduction and betrayal, as the old cliche goes, and expectation, or hope, and loss. I can see its attraction for a writer.

MALCOLM: As we speak, I'm now thinking about people who come to me. It doesn't all come from me and my interests. There's so much of this feeling out there, especially among the people who want to talk to journalists. In *In the Freud Archives*, Jeffrey Masson wanted to talk about how he'd been betrayed by the psychoanalytic establishment.

WACHTEL: Because he was initially hired to be the head of the archives, and then when he wanted to write his own view of Freud's . . . Maybe you could explain it.

MALCOLM: He had views that were not the views that the psychoanalytic establishment had. They kicked him out of his job and he wanted to tell me the story of his betrayal. And some of the other characters in that book, a man named Peter Swayle, also felt betrayed in some other respect. It's probably some kind of dovetailing of subject and interviewer that creates this pattern of my writing about betrayal.

WACHTEL: Then in the end, Jeffrey Masson felt betrayed by you, he ended up suing you for libel and defamation, though ultimately you won. Clearly he felt betrayed. Did you feel betrayed by his coming after you?

MALCOLM: No, I felt a little sheepish. I hadn't seen it coming, because that's very characteristic behavior. When he felt betrayed by his patron at the Freud archives, Kurt Eissler, he sued him, so this should not have been a piece of surprising behavior on his part. Usually when subjects feel betrayed, as Jeffrey Masson did, they find something else. Jeffrey Masson sued me not for betrayal but because he said I had misquoted him. And then I had to do a lot of work to show that I had not, and in that case had a little novelistic drama which hinged on some notes I had lost. I had only the typewritten version, and that was not as persuasive as the original notes would have been, and I finally did win a second trial, and a few years later, my little two-year-old granddaughter found the notebook—

WACHTEL: Oh really, I didn't hear that little coda to the story.

MALCOLM: Yes! The notes were found. The whole thing could've been avoided if that notebook had been put into a bookcase. I was in my country house, and there was something red on the floor, and I picked it up, this red notebook. My granddaughter had seen something red in the bookcase and pulled it out, and there were the notes. I felt like I was going to faint.

WACHTEL: So if you'd been on the jury—I'm asking a lot here—with *The Journalist and the Murderer*, do you know which way you would've gone? In terms of the murderer being betrayed by the journalist.

MALCOLM: Yeah, I probably would've said he was guilty of betrayal, if that's the charge. If there ever was betrayal. What interested me about this case is that it just seemed like a larger-than-life example of what goes on in every journalistic transaction. The journalist doesn't go so far as writing letters assuring the subject of something he then does the opposite of, but there's something down the ladder of that high treason that seemed worth looking at.

WACHTEL: Are you bothered by that aspect of the journalist-subject relationship in your own work?

MALCOLM: Sure, I think that's a problem for all journalists. And I've learned from looking at it that, for instance, one can narrow that gap of expectation by one's manner. One does not have to be as friendly as one would've thought you had to be. You can be quite neutral and don't raise the expectations, but it doesn't seem to make any difference. The subject goes on thinking you're there to tell their story. I've had the experience where after I wrote the book I would give subjects a copy of the book, sort of like a Miranda warning, but it didn't seem to make a difference.

WACHTEL: Miranda warning being the American [legal practice of] reading people their rights before they speak. [*laughs*] We've seen it on all the TV shows and everything. You've pointed out that biography and any nonfiction feels as real as the best fiction. Why is that?

MALCOLM: This is my own experience but I certainly get more involved with great works of fiction than I do with the great works of nonfiction. There's something more real, so to speak, about *War and Peace* and *Anna Karenina*.

WACHTEL: Because you can get that interiority, even though it's imagined?

MALCOLM: That's part of it, sure. There's no doubt about what happens there, there aren't alternate versions. When Tolstoy tells you something happened it really did happen, whereas in life it's much more ambiguous.

WACHTEL: We're flattened, or something.

MALCOLM: Maybe it's flattened because you know there's somebody else who can say, no it was a different way. In fiction, that's the paradox, there's only one way, and that's the way the author wrote it.

WACHTEL: Near the end of *The Journalist and the Murderer* you talk about how the characters of nonfiction come out of the writer's most idiosyncratic desires and deepest anxieties. Looking back on your book about Stein and Toklas, is it significant that while the American Stein and Toklas stayed in occupied Europe during the war, you and your family fled Czechoslovakia in 1939?

MALCOLM: I feel in a way in the same category as Stein and Toklas. I feel I was one of the rare lucky escapees from the Nazis, just by pure good luck. In that sense, I do identify with them. They are fellow lucky survivors.

WACHTEL: You were talking about the ambiguity inherent in the completeness of biography. What is its value to us? Well we're all curious. When we like something somebody has written or when we admire anybody we want to know about them, so it's a way of satisfying curiosity. I'm certainly not above reading biography even though I say these [*laughs*] nasty things about it.

MORE A CABINETMAKER THAN A TORMENTED ARTIST

INTERVIEW BY KATIE ROIPHE
THE PARIS REVIEW
SPRING 2011

Though I will make the trip up the elevator to Janet Malcolm's stately town-house apartment, overlooking Gramercy Park, three times in the course of this unusual interview, the substance of our exchange will take place by email, over three and a half months.

The reason for this is that Janet Malcolm is more naturally the describer than the described. It is nearly impossible to imagine the masterful interviewer chatting unguardedly into a tape recorder, and indeed she prefers not to imagine it. She has agreed to do the interview but only by email: in this way she has politely refused the role of subject and reverted to the more comfortable role of writer. She will be writing her answers—and, to be honest, tinkering gently with the phrasing of some of my questions.

So the true setting of this interview is not the book-lined walls of her living room, where we sit having mint tea, but screens: Malcolm's twenty-one-and-a-half-inch desktop Mac, with its worn white keyboard; my silver seventeen-inch MacBook, my iPad sometimes. The disadvantage of email is that it seems to breed a kind of formality, but the advantage is the familiarity of being in touch with someone over time. For us, this particular style of communication had the reassuring old-fashioned quality of considered correspondence; it is like Malcolm herself—careful, thorough, a bit elusive.

Malcolm was born in Prague, in 1934, and immigrated to this country when she was five. Her family lived with relatives in Flatbush, Brooklyn, for a year while her father, a psychiatrist and neurologist, studied for his medical boards, and then moved to Yorkville, in Manhattan. Malcolm attended the High School of Music and Art, and then went to the University of Michigan, where she began writing for the school paper, *The Michigan Daily*, and the humor magazine, *The Gargoyle*, which she later edited. In the years after college she moved to Washington with her husband, Donald Malcolm, and wrote occasional book reviews for *The New Republic*.

She and her husband moved to New York and, in 1963, had a daughter, Anne. That same year Malcolm's work first appeared in *The New Yorker*, where her husband, who died in 1975, was the off-Broadway critic. She began writing in what was then considered the woman's sphere: annual features on Christmas shopping and children's books, and a monthly column on design, called "About the House."

Later, Malcolm married her editor at *The New Yorker*, Gardner Botsford. She began to do the dense, idiosyncratic writing she is now known for when she quit smoking in 1978: she couldn't write without cigarettes, so she began reporting a long *New Yorker* fact piece, on family therapy, called "The One-Way Mirror." She set off for Philadelphia with a tape recorder—the old-fashioned kind, with tapes, which she uses to this day—and lined Mead composition notebooks with marbleized covers. By the time she finished the long period of reporting, she found she could finally write without smoking, and she had also found her form.

Her ten provocative books, including *The Journalist and the Murderer*, *Psychoanalysis: The Impossible Profession*, *The Silent Woman: Sylvia Plath and Ted Hughes*, *In the Freud Archives*, and *Two Lives: Gertrude and Alice*, are simultaneously beloved, demanding, scholarly, flashy, careful, bold, highbrow, and controversial. Many people have pointed out that her writing, which is often called journalism, is in fact some other wholly original form of art, some singular admixture of reporting, biography, literary criticism, psychoanalysis, and the nineteenth-century novel—English and Russian both. In one of the more colorful episodes of her long career, she was the defendant of a libel trial, brought by one of her subjects, Jeffrey Masson, in 1984; the courts ultimately found in her favor, in 1994, but the charges shadowed her for years, and both during the trial and afterward the journalistic community was not as supportive as one might have thought it would be.

In part this might be because Malcolm had already distanced herself from them. "Every journalist who is not too stupid or too full of himself to notice what is going on knows that what he does is morally indefensible," she wrote in the now-famous opening lines of *The Journalist and the Murderer*, and in much of her writing Malcolm delves into what she calls the "moral problem" of journalism. One of the most challenging or controversial elements of her work is her persistent and mesmerizing analysis of the relationship between the writer and her subject. ("Writing cannot be done in a state of desirelessness," she writes in *The Silent Woman*; and she exposes, over and over, the writer's prejudices and flaws, including her own.) When *The Journalist and the Murderer* came out in 1990, it created a stir in the literary world; it antagonized, in other words, precisely those people it was meant to antagonize. But it is now taught to nearly every undergraduate studying journalism, and Malcolm's fiery comment on the relationship between the journalist and her subject has been assimilated so completely into the larger culture that it has become a truism. Malcolm's work, then, occupies that strange glittering territory between controversy and the establishment: she is both a grande dame of journalism, and still, somehow, its enfant terrible.

Malcolm is admired for the fierceness of her satire, for the elegance of her writing, for the innovations of her form. She writes, in "A Girl of the Zeitgeist," an essay about the New York art world, "Perhaps even stronger than the room's aura of commanding originality is its sense of absences, its evocation of all the things that have been excluded, have been found wanting, have failed to capture the interest of Rosalind Krauss—which are most of the things in the world, the things of 'good taste' and fashion and consumerism, the things we see in stores and in one another's houses. No one can leave this loft without feeling a little rebuked: one's own house suddenly seems cluttered, inchoate, banal."

No living writer has narrated the drama of turning the messy and meaningless world into words as brilliantly, precisely, and analytically as Janet Malcolm. Whether she is writing about biography or a trial or psychoanalysis or Gertrude Stein, her story is the construction of the story, and her influence is so vast that much of the writing world has begun to think in the charged, analytic terms of a Janet Malcolm passage. She takes apart the official line, the accepted story, the court transcript like a mechanic takes apart a car engine, and shows us how it works; she narrates how the stories we tell ourselves are made from the vanities and jealousies and weaknesses of their players. This is her obsession, and no one can do it on her level.

Personally, though, she exhibits none of the flamboyance of her prose. Over the course of the interview, Malcolm appears to lack entirely the writer's natural exhibitionism, the writer's desire to talk endlessly about herself. If at all possible she will elegantly deflect the conversation away from her journalism to journalism in general; she will often quote, elude, glide over my question, responding instead to something she is comfortable answering. She is, not at all surprisingly, the kind of person who thinks through her revelations, who crafts and shines them so that the self revealed is as graceful and polished as one of her pieces.

Malcolm herself is slight, with glasses and intense brown eyes, something like Harriet the Spy would look like if she had grown to the venerable age of seventy-six and the world had showered her with the success she deserved. Her ambience is controlled, restrained, watchful. You will not, no matter how hard you try, be able to measure the effect of your words on her, and you will never be able to tell, even remotely, how she is reacting to anything you say. Around her it is hard not to feel large, flashy, blowsy, theatrical, reckless. Even though I ostensibly am interviewing her, I am still nervous about what impression I am making on her, still riveted and consumed by the idea of the three penetrating sentences she could make of me should she so desire.

Later, she will write to me, "Before I try to answer your question, I want to talk about that moment in our meeting at my apartment last week, when I left the room to find a book and suggested that while I was away you might want to take notes about the living room for the descriptive opening of this interview. Earlier you had made the distinction between writers for whom the physical world is significant and writers for whom it scarcely exists, who live in the world of ideas. You are clearly one of the latter. You obediently took out a notebook, and gave me a rather stricken look, as if I had asked you to do something faintly embarrassing."

I opened the notebook and took out a pen, but I already know that a large part of what is going on in the room, between the journalist, say, and the murderer, won't quite make it onto the page.

KATIE ROIPHE: I've often noticed how much work your physical descriptions do in your writing, how they make us feel we know and understand the subjects before they begin to speak, and how you impose your very singular interpretation in such an authoritative way that it feels organic, like anyone walking into a room couldn't help but see it exactly as you do. So how would you describe your apartment if you were the journalist walking into your living room?

JANET MALCOLM: My living room has an oakwood floor, Persian carpets, floor-to-ceiling bookcases, a large ficus and large fern, a fireplace with a group of photographs and drawings over it, a glass-top coffee table with a bowl of dried pomegranates on it, and sofas and chairs covered in off-white linen. If I were a journalist walking into the room, I would immediately start composing a satiric portrait of the New York writer's apartment with its standard tasteful objects (cat included) and general air of unrelenting Culture.

ROIPHE: Interesting, given my own blind spots with visual detail. I would have mentioned the cat, and maybe the decorative French dishes, and the view of the park, but I wouldn't have gone to satire. I guess if I were doing a close reading of the room I would have gotten "orderly and precise, carefully unpretentious, somehow perfect and comfortable." I got the impression of a room where no uncivilized scenes occur (revealing, I guess, more about myself than the room).

MALCOLM: You underestimate your powers of description. I admire "carefully unpretentious." That "carefully" has a nice sting. I'm not sure it's fully merited. The cat deserves some of the credit for the look of shabby chic—the stuffing that is coming out of the sofas and armchairs is entirely his doing. Did you notice the place where I pinned a patch over one of the most viciously clawed places? But, seriously, your generous and appreciative words only confirm my sense of the difficulty of autobiographical writing. If I had said these things about my living room ("somehow perfect and comfortable") I would have sounded conceited and complacent. The autobiographer works in a treacherous terrain. The journalist has a much safer job.

ROIPHE: It seems to me that for a journalist you use yourself, or the persona of "Janet Malcolm" anyway, more than most journalists. You use and analyze your own reaction to and relationship with many of your subjects, and often insert yourself into the drama. How is this "safer" than a more straightforward or autobiographical portrayal of self?

MALCOLM: This is a subject I've thought about a lot, and actually once wrote about—in the afterword to *The Journalist and the Murderer.* Here's what I said:

"The 'I' character in journalism is almost pure invention. Unlike the 'I' of autobiography, who is meant to be seen as a representation of the writer, the 'I' of journalism is connected to the writer only in a tenuous way—the way, say, that Superman is connected to Clark Kent. The journalistic 'I' is an overreliable narrator, a functionary to whom crucial tasks of narration and argument and tone have been entrusted, an ad hoc creation, like the chorus of Greek tragedy. He is an emblematic figure, an embodiment of the idea of the dispassionate observer of life."

It occurs to me now that the presence of this idealized figure in the narrative only compounds the inequality between writer and subject that is the moral problem of journalism as I see it. Compared to this wise and good person the other characters in the story—even the "good" ones—pale. The radiant persona of Joseph Mitchell, the great master of the journalistic "I," shines out of his works as perhaps no other journalist's does. In the old days at *The New Yorker*, every nonfiction writer tried to write like him, and, of course, none of us came anywhere near to doing so. This whole subject may be a good deal more complicated than I made it seem in the afterword. For one thing, Superman is connected to Clark Kent in a rather fundamental, if curious, way.

ROIPHE: I think that passage is lovely and convincing, but I wonder if that "I" as overreliable narrator is true of your journalism, or journalism in general. It seems to me that you very deliberately present yourself as something other than "the dispassionate observer." You often give yourself (or the character of Janet Malcolm in your work) flaws and vanities, and interrogate your own motives and reactions as fiercely as you interrogate other people's. I make no presumptions, of course, as to how close to you is the Janet Malcolm in your work—who envied Anne Stevenson at college, who is disappointed in Ingrid Sischy. But it does seem to me that the "I" in your work is very deliberately more Clark Kent than Superman.

MALCOLM: You're right that "dispassionate observer" doesn't properly describe the character I assume in my nonfiction writing—especially in the writing of recent years. When I first started doing long fact pieces, as they were called at *The New Yorker*, I modeled my "I" on the stock, civilized, and humane figure that was *The New Yorker* "I," but as I went along, I began to tinker with her and make changes in her personality. Yes, I gave her flaws and vanities and, perhaps most significantly, strong opinions. I had her take sides. I was influenced by this thing that was in the air called deconstruction. The idea I took from it was precisely the idea that there is no such thing as a dispassionate observer, that every narrative is inflected by the narrator's bias. Edward Said's

Orientalism made a great impression on me. And yes, probably this did add to the character's authority.

ROIPHE: Is it possible that your construction of an "I," and your method in general, is also influenced by psychoanalysis? You have chosen psychoanalysis as the subject of several of your books. How has it informed your voice and general approach?

MALCOLM: Although psychoanalysis has influenced me personally, it has had curiously little influence on my writing. This may be because writers learn from other writers, not from theories. But there are parallels between journalism and clinical psychoanalysis. Both the journalist and the psychoanalyst are connoisseurs of the small, unregarded motions of life. Both pan the surface—yes, surface—for the gold of insight. The metaphor of depth—as in depth psychology—is wrong, as the psychoanalyst Roy Schafer helpfully pointed out. The unconscious is right there on the surface, as in "The Purloined Letter." Journalism, with its mandate to notice small things, was always congenial to me. I might also have liked being an analyst. But I never would have gotten into medical school, because I couldn't do math, so it wasn't an option. I never went to journalism school, either. When I started doing journalism, a degree from a journalism school wasn't considered necessary. In fact, it was considered a little tacky.

ROIPHE: Interesting. I do wonder, though, if psychoanalysis might be somehow involved in your unearthing of the hidden aggressions involved in the writing process. One of the most striking elements of your work is the preoccupation with the relationship between the writer and her subject. In a recent *New Yorker* piece, you say of journalism that "malice remains its animating impulse." This type of motive searching seems to me to be somehow connected to the habits of mind we associate with psychoanalysis.

MALCOLM: I think you are asking me, in the most tactful way possible, about my own aggression and malice. What can I do but plead guilty? I don't know whether journalists are more aggressive and malicious than people in other professions. We are certainly not a "helping profession." If we help anyone, it is ourselves, to what our subjects don't realize they are letting us take. I am hardly the first writer to have noticed the not-niceness of journalists. Tocqueville wrote about the despicableness of American journalists in *Democracy in America*. In Henry James's satiric novel *The Reverberator*, a wonderful rascally journalist named George M. Flack appears. I am only one of many contributors to this critique. I am also not the only journalist contributor. Tom Wolfe and Joan Didion, for instance, have written on the subject. Of course, being aware of your rascality doesn't excuse it.

ROIPHE: I wonder if you are subtly separating yourself from the herd of journalists who don't examine or reflect on the matter, as Didion does with that line that suggests that talking to journalists runs counter to one's best interests. When you admit to your rascality, it certainly creates the impression that you are being honest in a way that readers are not accustomed to in their journalists and critics.

MALCOLM: When I wrote *The Journalist and the Murderer*, I guess I was (not all that subtly) separating myself from the herd of journalists, and a lot of them got mad at me for breaking ranks. There was something deeply irritating about this woman who set herself up as being more honest and clear-sighted than anyone else. My analysis of journalistic betrayal was seen as a betrayal of journalism itself as well as a piece of royal chutzpah. Today, my critique seems obvious, even banal. No one argues with it, and, yes, it has degenerated—as critiques do—into a sort of lame excuse.

ROIPHE: Much of your work concerns court cases and trials. Can you explain what it is about legal proceedings that interests you, and in what particular ways they lend themselves to your kind of writing?

MALCOLM: Trials offer exceptional opportunities for the exercise of journalistic heartlessness. The antagonists in trials lend themselves to the kind of cold scrutiny that few people can withstand. Trial transcripts are cruel documents. The court stenographer dutifully records everything she hears and what appears on the page often reads like something from the theater of the absurd. The court scenes in *The Journalist and the Murderer* and *The Crime of Sheila McGough* are based entirely on transcripts. I wrote about the trials after they were over. It is only in my new book, *Iphigenia in Forest Hills*, that I wrote about a trial I actually attended. But I also relied heavily on the transcript. One of the most interesting parts of a trial are the sotto voce sidebars or bench conferences in

which the attorneys and judge take off the masks they have
put on for the jury and spectators. These conferences are re-
corded by the court stenographer and appear in the transcript,
to which they often contribute a note of high comedy.

ROIPHE: Do you ever read thrillers? Courtroom dramas?
Mysteries?

MALCOLM: Your question brings to mind Edmund Wilson's
essay with the wonderful title "Who Cares Who Killed Roger
Ackroyd?" and I have just reread it. It's in the collection Classics and Commercials. Wilson despised detective fiction. He
had written a previous put-down of the genre called "Why Do
People Read Detective Stories?" which "brought me letters of
protest in a volume and of a passionate earnestness which had
hardly been elicited even by my occasional criticisms of the
Soviet Union." (Wilson was writing in 1945.) The protesting
letter writers told him he had not read the right detective novels, so he went and read Dorothy Sayers and Margery Allingham and Raymond Chandler and others—who bored and
repelled him even more than Rex Stout and Agatha Christie
had. "The reading of detective stories is simply a kind of vice
that, for silliness and minor harmfulness, ranks somewhere
between smoking and crossword puzzles," he wrote. I first
read Wilson in the fifties and took his pronouncements very
much to heart, as many other writers-to-be of my generation
did. He was (and remains) a writer of tremendous authority.
After reading "Who Cares Who Killed Roger Ackroyd?" it
was years before it occurred to me to determine the answer

for myself. I eventually came to like a number of the writers he hated, though his dim view of Dorothy Sayers stuck.

ROIPHE: I am curious which writers you came to like that he hated. Many critics have commented on the thriller-like pacing or detective-story suspense of your journalism. You manage to infuse a sort of page-turning energy into subjects that might otherwise be dry or academic, like the Freud archives or biography writing. Is there anything you have consciously taken from mysteries or thrillers, in terms of pacing, or is there some other way to account for this quality in your work? Is there any other fiction that influences your journalism? What novels do you like to read?

MALCOLM: I am puzzling about how to answer your question. I can't think of anything I have consciously taken from mysteries and thrillers, but maybe I have been influenced unconsciously. The mystery writers that Wilson hated that I came to like were Margery Allingham, Ngaio Marsh, and Agatha Christie. What novels do I like to read? I love the great nineteenth-century English, American, and Russian novels and short stories. Jane Austen, George Eliot, Trollope, Dickens, James, Hawthorne, Melville, Tolstoy, and Chekhov are among my favorites. Among twentieth-century novelists and short-story writers, there are Proust, Dreiser, Fitzgerald, Nabokov, Updike, Roth, and Alice Munro. I can't imagine a nonfiction writer who wasn't influenced by the fiction he or she had read. But the "thriller-like pacing" you find in my writing may come more from my own beat than from thrillers. I walk fast and am impatient. I get bored easily—no less with my own ideas than with those of others. Writing for me is a process of constantly throwing out stuff that doesn't seem interesting enough. I grew up in a family of big interrupters.

ROIPHE: Your journalism has the rich descriptions and characterizations that we associate with fiction, especially nineteenth-century fiction, as well as the storytelling qualities of a novel. In your wonderful piece on Vanessa Bell in *The New Yorker*, you write that you have conveniently forgotten that you are not writing a novel. Have you ever written fiction?

MALCOLM: I tried writing fiction in high school and college, the way bookish kids did then and perhaps still do. In college—the University of Michigan—I took a creative-writing course with the novelist Allan Seager, who gave me a C for the term. It was mortifying but probably helpful. I never tried to write fiction again. A kinder teacher might have permitted me to delude myself about my abilities as a short-story writer. Seager's brutal frankness probably spared me a lot of hopeless effort. I can report, but I cannot invent. What nonfiction writers take from novelists and short-story writers (as well as from other nonfiction writers) are the devices of narration. Made-up and true stories are narrated in the same way. There's an art to it. But I'm not all that conscious of what I am doing as I do it. I just know that something has to be done to turn my notes into a readable text. This something is what you teach, isn't it?

ROIPHE: This is what I teach, and that's why I am a little shocked by the story about the fiction class. But I am interested in your use of the phrase "brutal frankness" for this probably misguided teacher. It seems to me that you use that phrase admiringly, and that you admire a kind of frankness that you also perceive as brutal. Am I right? And can you explain your relation to that particular mode of perception?

MALCOLM: That is such an interesting observation. It never occurred to me that "brutal frankness" was such a charged phrase. Of course it is. But it takes someone of your generation to look at it askance. At the time of Allan Seager's C— the early fifties—a male chauvinist teacher like Seager (he clearly preferred the boys in the class) was nothing unusual. I came to feminism late. Women who came of age at the time that I did developed aggressive ways to attract the notice of the superior males. The habit of attention getting stays with you. This is just a stab at trying to answer your question, but perhaps it makes sense? Here is something else: during my four years of college I didn't study with a single woman professor. There weren't any, as far as I know.

ROIPHE: Tell me more about this attention-getting habit. It's not a hundred percent clear to me what you mean.

MALCOLM: It's not a hundred percent clear to me, either. In that piece about Vanessa Bell you mentioned earlier, I quote a young Virginia Woolf on the subject of her gay friends. What she called "the society of buggers" has "many advantages— if you are a woman," she wrote in a memoir called "Old Bloomsbury." "It is simple, it is honest, it makes one feel . . . in some respects at one's ease." But "it has this drawback— with buggers one cannot, as nurses say, show off. Something is always suppressed, held down. Yet this showing off, which is not copulating, necessarily, nor altogether being in love, is one of the great delights, one of the chief necessities of life." Showing off to straight men remained a delight and necessity to women of my generation. Those of us who wrote, wrote for men and showed off to them. Our writing had a certain note. I'm not sure I can describe it, but I can hear it. You have led us into deep waters. This is a complex and murky subject. Perhaps we can cut through the haze together.

ROIPHE: I wonder if part of that note you are talking about is a kind of dazzling sharpness. George Bernard Shaw wrote that Rebecca West wielded a pen as brilliantly as he and "much more savagely," and H. G. Wells said that she "wrote like God." Along those same lines, Elizabeth Hardwick writes about how Mary McCarthy is not constrained by feminine "niceness." Is that fierceness in both West and McCarthy, and even, say, Susan Sontag, part of what you mean by that "showing off" and that "certain note"? Is there something about being a woman writer in a very male field that leads to a kind of brilliant aggression on the page?

MALCOLM: The aggression is coupled with flirtation. That way you get the guys to say you write like God. Maybe we should move on to a new subject.

ROIPHE: How about editing? Have you had editors you liked working with? Can you tell me about how you edit your own work, and the welcome or unwelcome editing from the outside world?

MALCOLM: I'm so glad you've asked this question, because it allows me to correct an omission. When I answered your question about the pace of my writing I should have gone on to mention someone with an even shorter attention span than my own, namely, my husband, the late Gardner Botsford, who was my editor at *The New Yorker*. By way of answering your question about editing, let me quote some things I said about Gardner at his memorial service in 2005:

He hated it when people went on and on. Much of his work as an editor was devoted to the elimination of superfluous words—often of superfluous paragraphs—sometimes even of superfluous pages. . . He did many other things as well—his taste, his ear for language, his passion for clarity were apparent in each of his editorial interventions. I remember the first time I was edited by him. I read the page proof that was the result of the many pencil marks he had made on my manuscript, and I felt the kind of pleasure one feels when coming upon a wonderful painting or on hearing a gorgeous aria. In the most dazzlingly deft way, without in any way changing its meaning, Gardner had transformed bumpy writing into polished prose. Over the years, I became more blasé about his editing, as one does about indoor plumbing, but I treasure the memory of my first encounter with its almost uncanny delicacy and potency. A. J. Liebling put it most bluntly and best when he said to Gardner—whose editing he had at first stubbornly resisted and finally gratefully accepted—"You make me sound like a real writer."

Manuscripts have been preserved with Gardner's markings on them, and on first sight it looks as if someone had taken an axe to a helpless piece of writing. But on closer scrutiny, you see the tact with which each intervention was made. Gardner always said that an editor's first obligation was to the reader, but he had a remarkable feeling for every writer's form of expression, so that his changes on behalf of the reader always read as if the writer rather than some crass interloper were making them. If Gardner were here, I don't think he would disagree with what I have said, but chances are he would be looking at his watch.

ROIPHE: I think that is the most romantic or lovely account of editing I have ever encountered. Is it difficult to write without him? I know with some of my great editors, I sometimes think of what they would say in my head as I am writing. Do you have that relationship with his editing?

MALCOLM: Yes, I do. When Gardner was alive I wrote more sloppily than I do today; I knew he would be there to clean up after me. Now I try to pick up after myself as I go along. But I am hardly without help. I have a brilliant editor at *The New Yorker*, Ann Goldstein, who has the ear for language and delicate pencil that Gardner had. I depend on her for what I depended on Gardner for: she puts the same shine on sentences that he did. Where Gardner is irreplaceable— where Ann and I can only try to equal him—is in his fearless cutting and rearranging. One writer at *The New Yorker*, who was too in love with every word he wrote to get the point of Gardner's editing, called him "The Ripper." I would get Gardner's point most of the time, though here and there—rightly or wrongly—I disagreed with him, but not often.

ROIPHE: Could you say a bit about the mechanics of your writing process? Do you work regular hours or in bursts of inspiration? Do you edit yourself? Do you approach writing in a workmanlike way? Are you are a cabinetmaker making a cabinet, or is there more drama or torment?

MALCOLM: I'm definitely more a cabinetmaker than a tormented artist. Not that writing comes easy. I don't know about cabinetmakers, but I often get stuck. Then I get sleepy and have to lie down. Or I make myself leave the house—walking sometimes produces a solution. The problem is usually one of logic or point of view. I keep regular morning hours. The first hour is the most productive one. The two or three others are less so—they can even be completely fruitless. I sometimes work in the afternoon as well, but the morning is the obligatory work time. As for the "mechanics" of composition, all I can say about them is that the machinery works slowly and erratically and I am always a little nervous about it, though by now I'm pretty used to it. I guess I trust it more.

As for self-editing: when I turn in a piece, I expect that there will be suggestions for changes, and I am not bad at using these suggestions to improve the text. But I need the hint that something isn't right.

ROIPHE: Are there any of your books that you found harder to write than the others?

MALCOLM: I found the world of *The Crime of Sheila Mc-Gough* harder to enter than those of any other of my other books. It was the world of business fraud. It was a great struggle for me to grasp the intricacies of the fraud I was writing about. I resented studying such a stupid subject. I felt I could have learned German or flamenco dancing in the time I spent trying to get a handle on the crooked business deals of a con man named Bob Bailes. Sheila McGough was his lawyer and his victim, in the sense that she was accused and convicted of being his coconspirator. In fact she was just a strangely over-zealous advocate. She was an innocent Catholic girl who lived with her aged parents and didn't have a dishonest bone in her body. But a skillful prosecutor was able to persuade the jury of her guilt. The book was the least successful of my books. I have many boxfuls of it in my basement. I happen to like it a lot—perhaps the way you like the runt of the litter. But it may be that readers didn't want to be in this world, either. I may not have succeeded in getting the tedium out of it. Then again, I may have.

ROIPHE: Which of your books, in contrast, came the most naturally?

MALCOLM: I don't recall having any special trouble with my latest book, *Iphigenia in Forest Hills*. But—to quote the title of Nora Ephron's new book—I remember nothing.

ROIPHE: In *Iphigenia in Forest Hills*, it seems that the logic of the plot is leading to the idea that Mazoltuv Borukhova received an unfair trial, and might be innocent, and yet at the end you don't seem to think she is innocent. Did you think she was innocent at any point, or did you want her to be innocent? She's altogether a fascinating character, at the center of the book. Can you talk a little bit about how you felt about her as you were writing?

MALCOLM: Somewhere in the book I write that "Borukhova's otherness was her defining characteristic." As I went along I felt I understood her less and less. She seemed more and more alien, as did her sisters and mother. I had hoped to interview her but was never able to. She was like a wild animal who couldn't be lured into the have-a-heart trap. Both her defense lawyer and her appeals lawyer held out the possibility of an interview, but it never happened. So there is a kind of hole in the center of the book. She becomes who you imagine she is. The prosecutor led the jurors to imagine her as a thoroughly bad person. The defense lawyer did not succeed in substituting a different characterization. Her appearance on the stand only permitted the prosecutor to flesh out his portrait of her as an evil liar. His was a heartlessly lethal trap.

ROIPHE: I certainly see what you mean that she is a cipher who becomes whoever you imagine her to be (not unlike Sylvia Plath in *The Silent Woman*). But it seems from your language here that you have some sympathy for her. I guess my question is, what would you have done if you were on the jury? And did you feel some sympathy for her otherness, for her being, as you say—and it definitely came across in the book—an animal in a trap?

MALCOLM: I felt great sympathy for her as a mother. But I was puzzled by her willingness to accept the judge's terrible ruling that her child go live with the father she feared. In her situation, I would have defied the order. I would have taken my child and gone to live in another state or country under an assumed name. I think I would have. None of us knows for sure what we are capable of, how we will behave when tested.

What would I have done if I had been on the jury? I think I would have voted for acquittal. The ninety telephone calls connected Borukhova to Mallayev—who does seem to have done it—but did not conclusively prove that she had hired him to kill her husband. It looked as if she had, but is that enough? The prosecutor evidently thought it wasn't—that to get his conviction he needed to blacken her character. Verdicts are not reached in a state of detachment. My interviews with two of the jurors showed how much their verdict was determined by their dislike of her and their wish to find her guilty.

ROIPHE: In the book you attribute at least some of Borukhova's mysterious "otherness" to her being part of an immigrant community and being new to the system, so to speak. Obviously you are from a very different world, but I wonder whether coming to this country as a child gave you any sense of otherness, or if you think that experience, of having to take in new systems, in any way affected your identity as a writer.

MALCOLM: I came here at the age of five and knew no

English. Many of the memories I have of the time are about my confusions and misperceptions in a kindergarten in Brooklyn to which my parents had casually and probably unwisely sent me. For example, there was a class trip from which I was excluded because I hadn't grasped in time that I was supposed to bring money from home in order to go on it. Another memory is of the kindergarten teacher saying, "Good-bye, children," at the end of the day, and my envy of the girl whose name I assumed to be "Children." It was my secret hope that someday the teacher would say, "Good-bye, Janet." I have never connected these pathetic struggles with a language I didn't know to later struggles with the language I tried and try not to disgrace myself in as a professional writer, but there may be a connection after all. Your question gives me much to think about.

ROIPHE: To return, for a moment, to what you were saying about Borukhova as a mother: Did you find having a child a conflict with your writing? It may be telling that I am keeping a list, but I've noticed that all of the women writers I most admire have had no children, or at the most, only one. I wonder if you ever felt a pull between ambition and the child, if the ruthlessness of the writer was ever in conflict with the instincts of the mother?

MALCOLM: I have indeed felt the pull between the ruthlessness of the writer and the instincts of the mother. But this may be too deep a subject for an email exchange on the art of nonfiction. Probably the place to discuss our struggles with the art of mothering is a dark bar.

ROIPHE: You're probably right. I notice in your answers to my questions a kind of collage element. You will often paste in long quotations, and that is also true of your nonfiction and criticism. Can you explain your attraction to this technique?

MALCOLM: Well, the most obvious attraction of quotation is that it gives you a little vacation from writing—the other person is doing the work. All you have to do is type. But there is a reason beyond sloth for my liking of quotation at length. It permits you to show the thing itself rather than the pale, and never quite right, simulacrum that paraphrase is. For this reason I prefer books of letters to biographies. I am tempted to quote myself on this subject—I wrote about it in the Vanessa Bell piece we talked about earlier—but you have made me feel self-conscious, maybe even a little guilty, about this practice, so I will resist the impulse.

ROIPHE: Can you tell me about your interviewing style? How do you elicit stories from your subjects, and what have you observed over the years about interviewing in general, and about how people respond to journalists' questions?

MALCOLM: I wrote about this in *The Journalist and the Murderer*. A *Newsday* reporter named Bob Keeler had given me a book containing the transcripts of his interviews with Joe McGinniss and Jeffrey MacDonald, prefaced by lists of the questions he planned to ask.

When I got home, I leafed through the book and put it aside. I had not asked for it, and I felt there was something almost illicit about having it in my possession. To read

Keeler's interviews would be like eavesdropping on someone else's conversation, and to use anything from them would be like stealing. Above all—and cutting much deeper than any concern about eavesdropping and stealing—was the affront to my pride. An interview, after all, is only as good as the journalist who conducts it, and I felt—to put it bluntly—that Keeler, with his prepared questions and his newspaper reporter's directness, would not get from his subjects the kind of authentic responses that I try to elicit from mine with a more Japanese technique. When I finally read Keeler's transcripts, however, I was in for a surprise and an illumination. MacDonald and McGinniss had said exactly the same things to the unsubtle Keeler that they had said to me. It hadn't made the slightest difference that Keeler had read from a list of prepared questions and I had acted as if I were passing the time of day. From Keeler's blue book I learned the same truth about subjects that the analyst learns about patients: they will tell their story to anyone who will listen to it, and the story will not be affected by the behavior or personality of the listener; just as ("good enough") analysts are interchangeable, so are journalists.

As you must be thinking, I am reverting to my habit of self-quotation—and perhaps enacting the "truth" of the passage? I put in the question mark, because I'm suddenly not all that sure about any of this. After my book came out, several readers wrote and asked, "What is the Japanese technique?" Perhaps I underestimated its power. Some part of your persona is surely hovering over this interview and affecting if not shaping my answers.

ROIPHE: Let me ask you a question you might think is unrelated. I love the passage in *BUtterfield 8* where John O'Hara writes that Gloria's outgoing, butterflyish adult personality is a compensation for being a shy child. Were you a shy child?

MALCOLM: Yes, I was. But you've met me. Do I really strike you as outgoing and butterflyish?

ROIPHE: Well, no. But the formalized social aggression of the reporter does seem in its own way a manifestation of "outgoing." I also wonder: Do you carry your journalist's scrutiny and habits into normal social life, say, at a party or a lunch, or are they confined to the interview situation?

MALCOLM: I think I'm pretty much the same all the time. I don't talk a lot and I look as if I'm interested in what people are saying. Of course, this isn't always the case. I like to use a tape recorder when I interview—mainly to capture the interviewee's characteristic habits of speech, but also because it allows me to let my mind wander and later recover the interesting things he or she may have said. At lunches and parties there is no second chance for the daydreamer.

ROIPHE: You write in *The Silent Woman* that the subject and the interviewer "are always being distracted and seduced by the encounter's outward resemblance to an ordinary friendly meeting." Do you feel that distraction and seduction as an interviewer, or have you moved beyond that?

MALCOLM: One day last year during Passover I spent a lot of time at the Whole Foods store trying to decide which of their packaged kosher cookies to bring to the house of the Bukharan Jewish family I was interviewing that night. I wanted to bring something nice and none of the cookies looked great, but there was nothing else suitable. When I got home, I examined the packages of cookies and thought of going back and exchanging the chocolate bark, which looked particularly unappetizing, for more macaroons. Then I thought that maybe it would be better—more "professional"—not to bring anything. I consulted a friend, who said decisively, "You can't visit a Jewish family and not bring anything." So I brought the cookies to the interview. Throughout the evening I was distracted by the question of whether the mother of the house would open the packages and pass around the cookies.

I think that one never completely moves beyond the pull of the personal in any human encounter. But I think that when journalists remember that the interview is a special sort of encounter, and withhold some of their natural friendliness, they don't lose anything by it. The subject doesn't notice. He wants to tell his story. And when the journalist retells the story in a way the subject cannot anticipate, he doesn't feel like such a rat.

ROIPHE: Can you analyze a little the response in the world of writers and journalists to the libel trial that was brought against you and *The New Yorker* by Jeffrey Masson? It seems to me surprising that the larger community didn't rally to support you in a more emphatic way. You wrote later that you found the notebook that contained the handwritten version of some of the quotations he claimed you fabricated, in your country house, while your granddaughter was playing near a bookcase. I still occasionally hear people saying they don't believe you found the notebook, or who believe there was no libel but have some vague sense there was some tricky journalistic wrongdoing. Why do you think people, especially journalists, reacted the way they did?

MALCOLM: When I wrote *The Journalist and the Murderer*, I did so in the, as it proved, foolish belief that Jeffrey Masson's lawsuit against me and *The New Yorker*—which had been dismissed by a California court—was permanently over. I should have known, having written his portrait, that Masson wouldn't give up so easily. He appealed, and soon after the two-part *New Yorker* article came out as a book he succeeded in overturning the decision and getting his day in court. The journalistic community, which (as I noted earlier) was irritated with me for my remarks about journalism, was naturally delighted by this turn of events. Who could blame it? Who hasn't felt pleasure in the fall of the self-styled mighty? That it was a *New Yorker* writer who was being dragged through the mud only added to the wicked joy. At that time, the magazine was still wrapped in a fluffy cocoon of moral superiority that really got up the noses of people who worked at other publications. I didn't help myself by behaving the way writers at *The New Yorker* thought they ought to behave when approached by the press: like little replicas of the publicity-phobic William Shawn. So instead of defending myself against the false accusations Masson made in interview after interview, I maintained my ridiculous silence. Eventually I was able to convince a jury that I was telling the truth and had not made anything up. But by refusing to tell my side of the story to the press, by acting as if I didn't have to tell my side of the story, since who could doubt its truth, I lost in the court of public opinion.

Another mistake I made was to take the lesson of *Jarndyce v. Jarndyce* to heart and pay as little attention as possible to Masson's lawsuit; I thought, "Let the lawyers handle it and I will live my life and do my work and not end up like those miserable court-obsessed wretches in *Bleak House*." But this was the wrong lesson. Years later I realized that the lawyers had mishandled the case. They had got it dismissed— through a legal mechanism called summary judgment—on grounds that I would never have consented to if I had been paying attention. The judge granted my lawyer's plea that the three quotations at issue (for which I had lost my handwritten notes) were so similar to quotations that were on tape that even if they had been made up, Masson still didn't have a case. This is completely wrong! (As the Supreme Court rightly saw.) "Similar" is not "same." In the press, the "even if" got translated into a "that is so"—into an admission of guilt. I am not surprised to hear that there are people who still think I did something wrong.

One final thought about the lawsuit. It was not pleasant to be sued and it was painful to be pilloried by my fellow journalists, but it was an experience I wouldn't have missed. It wasn't life threatening, and it was deeply interesting. It took me out of a sheltered place and threw me into bracingly icy water. What more could a writer want?

THE LAST
INTERVIEW

THE NEW YORK TIMES BOOK REVIEW
FEBRUARY 14, 2019

WHAT BOOKS ARE ON YOUR NIGHTSTAND?

JANET MALCOLM: I take it you mean the imaginary Doric column that supports a teetering pile of current and old books that the interviewee wants to bring to the reader's attention. My actual nightstand is a small wood table with a box of Kleenex, a two-year-old Garnet Hill catalog and a cough drop on it. When I go to bed I bring with me the book I am reading during the day. Right now it is the British edition of Sally Rooney's brilliant, enigmatic new novel, *Normal People*.

HOW DO YOU ORGANIZE YOUR BOOKS?

MALCOLM: I organize them by genre. The largest section is fiction, which I alphabetize. I also alphabetize poetry. The other sections—biography, autobiography, theater, philosophy, anthropology, sociology, history, classical literature, literary criticism, art, photography, books by friends—are not alphabetized. I can find my way around them. I have been doing a lot of rereading in recent years. Why have a large library and not use it? Why keep books, if you are not going to read them more than once? For the décor? The answer isn't entirely no. A book-lined room looks nice. I like walking into my living room and seeing the walls of books with faded spines that have accreted over many decades.

WHAT BOOK MIGHT PEOPLE BE SURPRISED TO FIND ON YOUR SHELVES?

MALCOLM: *Our Princesses and Their Dogs* by Michael Chance, which was given to me by my British son-in-law for Christmas a few years ago. People who know me associate me with cats rather than dogs, but in this case that has no bearing on the book's prominent place in my heart. It was published in 1936, when the princesses' uncle Edward had not yet abdicated and their dad was just Bertie, Duke of York. But it is almost as if the author could see into the future and recognize the family's special monarchical fitness. Its benign charisma wafts out from delicate black-and-white photographs, and from a text that can only be read—if it is not to be found entirely risible—as an allegory of the relation of royalty to its people. Chance writes largely from the points of view of the family's happy dogs—two corgis named Dookie and Lady Jane, three Labradors named Mimsy, Stiffy and Scrummy, a Tibetan lion dog named Choo-choo, a golden retriever named Judy and a cocker spaniel named Ben—pausing only to praise the owners for being "not merely people who love dogs but warmhearted, human people who, understanding their animals, are therefore understood by them in return." At nine, Elizabeth already has the kindly placidity of the queen she is to become. Five-year-old Margaret steals the show with her mischievous charm. Margaret's adult life of petulant desperation, mordantly chronicled in Craig Brown's 2018 book *Ninety-Nine Glimpses of Princess Margaret,* could not have been foreseen in a million years by readers of *Our Princesses and Their Dogs.*

WHAT BOOKS WOULD YOU RECOMMEND TO SOMEONE WHO WANTS TO KNOW MORE ABOUT AMERICAN CULTURE?

MALCOLM: *Democracy in America* by Alexis de Tocqueville, *Adventures of Huckleberry Finn* by Mark Twain, and *The Other America* by Michael Harrington.

WHICH WRITERS–NOVELISTS, PLAYWRIGHTS, CRITICS, JOURNALISTS, POETS–WORKING TODAY DO YOU ADMIRE MOST?

MALCOLM: The poet Louise Glück, the short story writer Alice Munro, the journalist/essayist Ian Frazier, the journalist/biographer Calvin Tomkins, the critic Sharon Cameron, the journalist/essayist Michael Greenberg, the art historian Michael Fried. May I stretch your "working today" criteria to include Richard Wilbur and Philip Roth, who, in the eye of eternity, were still working the day before yesterday?

DISAPPOINTING, OVERRATED, JUST NOT GOOD: WHAT BOOK DID YOU FEEL AS IF YOU WERE SUPPOSED TO LIKE AND DIDN'T?

MALCOLM: Barack Obama's *Dreams from My Father.* It is good or good enough ("You're likable enough, Hillary") but it isn't Rousseau's *Confessions* or Gosse's *Father and Son*. The extravagant praise it received seemed excessive to me. Obama himself is another matter. I came to intensely admire and appreciate him over the years of his presidency. I believe he is a great man.

WHAT KIND OF READER WERE YOU AS A CHILD?

MALCOLM: An avid reader, to use Robert Gottlieb's wonderful phrase. I read everything in sight. I read the Grimm fairy tales, *Heidi, Little Women, Emily of New Moon, Little Lord Fauntleroy, The Snow Queen*; I went to the library every week and took out the four books you were allowed to borrow. I liked contemporary romantic novels with hints of sex ("he unbuttoned the top two buttons of her blouse"). My father would give my sister and me classics for birthdays and Christmas—*The Hunchback of Notre Dame, Les Misérables, David Copperfield* among them. I didn't differentiate between the adult masterpieces, the cheesy adult books and the children's classics. Bookish children are not critics. They just like to read.

WHAT DO YOU PLAN TO READ NEXT?

MALCOLM: I plan to go back to *Bleak House*, which I put aside during the holidays. It was like a boulder that was standing in the way of shorter books that were in the house, tempting me with their bigger type and smaller ambition. For example, Alexander McCall Smith's cozy (though by no means trivial) new No. 1 Ladies' Detective Agency novel, *The Colors of All the Cattle*. Now I am ready to return to the wild terrain of Dickens's great work.

WHO IS YOUR FAVORITE FICTIONAL HERO OR HEROINE? YOUR FAVORITE ANTIHERO OR VILLAIN?

MALCOLM: I love all of Jane Austen's major heroines—Lizzie Bennet, Fanny Price, Emma Woodhouse, Anne Elliot and Elinor Dashwood—and one of Tolstoy's heroes, Prince Andrei. I also very much like Ántonia Shimerda, the heroine of Willa Cather's *My Ántonia*. A favorite antihero or villain? There are none. I follow the author's direction to despise him or her. On second thought, I must confess to a sneaking liking for the antiheroine Lizzie Eustace—as Trollope himself surely had.

WHICH GENRES DO YOU ESPECIALLY ENJOY READING? AND WHICH DO YOU AVOID?

MALCOLM: I like books in the genre that could be described as the bee-in-your-bonnet genre, books in which the author has an obsessive thesis, and argues it so brilliantly that you come away completely convinced and elated by the erudition that has powered the argument. Some examples are: Edward Said's *Orientalism*, Leo Steinberg's *The Sexuality of Christ in Renaissance Art and in Modern Oblivion*, Ted Hughes's *Shakespeare and the Goddess of Complete Being* and Edgar Wind's *Pagan Mysteries in the Renaissance*. Among the genres I avoid are books on bodybuilding and moneymaking.

WHAT'S THE LAST BOOK YOU RECOMMENDED TO SOMEONE IN YOUR FAMILY?

MALCOLM: The thirteen-volume edition of Anton Chekhov's stories translated by Constance Garnett.

WHEN DO YOU READ?

MALCOLM: All the time.

JANET MALCOLM was born in Prague in 1934. Her family immigrated to the United States when she was five and lived in Brooklyn and then Manhattan, New York. After attending the High School of Music and Art, Malcolm matriculated at the University of Michigan, where she wrote for the school paper, *The Michigan Daily,* and the humor magazine, *The Gargoyle*. Upon graduating, she married Donald Malcolm and moved to Washington, DC, where she began to occasionally write book reviews for *The New Republic.* In 1963, she published her first piece in *The New Yorker.* Her husband, who had begun serving as the off-Broadway critic at *The New Yorker,* passed away in 1975. She married her editor at *The New Yorker,* Gardner Botsford (1917–2004), that year, and three years later she wrote her first piece in the style that would characterize the rest of her career. She went on to publish her first book, *Psychoanalysis: The Impossible Profession,* in 1981. She continued to contribute regularly to *The New Yorker* and wrote seven more books, including *The Journalist and Murderer, In the Freud Archives,* and *The Silent Woman*. She died on June 16, 2021, in New York Presbyterian Hospital.

DAPHNE BEAL is the author of the novel *In the Land of No Right Angles* and numerous essays, articles, and short stories. Her work has appeared in *The New York Times Magazine, Vogue, McSweeney's, Open City,* and *The London Review of Books,* among other publications.

NAN GOLDBERG has written and edited for numerous newspapers and magazines, including the *Boston Globe, The Forward, Salon, The New York Observer,* the *New York Post, The Star-Ledger, The Jerusalem Post,* and *The Atlantic Monthly*. She writes about authors and books—literature and nonfiction both. She has interviewed, among many others: Renata Adler, Alan Dershowitz, Nathan Englander, bell hooks, Norman Mailer, Queen Noor of Jordan, Cynthia Ozick, Anna Deavere Smith, Calvin Trillin, and Scott Turow.

KATIE ROIPHE is an American author and journalist. Her books include *The Power Notebooks, In Praise of Messy Lives,* and *The Violet Hour*. She is the director of the Cultural Reporting and Criticism program at New York University.

ELEANOR WACHTEL is a Canadian writer and broadcaster. She has been the host of the flagship literary show Writers & Company on CBC Radio One since its inception in 1990. In 2004, she was named to the Order of Canada, and in 2014 she was promoted from Member to Officer.

THE LAST INTERVIEW SERIES

JOHN LEWIS:
THE LAST INTERVIEW

$16.99 / $22.99 CAN

978-1-61219-962-7
ebook: 978-1-61219-963-4

FRIDA KAHLO:
THE LAST INTERVIEW

$16.99 / $22.99 CAN

978-1-61219-875-0
ebook: 978-1-61219-876-7

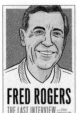

FRED ROGERS:
THE LAST INTERVIEW

$16.99 / $21.99 CAN

978-1-61219-895-8
ebook: 978-1-61219-896-5

TONI MORRISON:
THE LAST INTERVIEW

$16.99 / $22.99 CAN

978-1-61219-873-6
ebook: 978-1-61219-874-3

SHIRLEY CHISHOLM:
THE LAST INTERVIEW

$16.99 / $22.99 CAN

978-1-61219-897-2
ebook: 978-1-61219-898-9

GRAHAM GREENE:
THE LAST INTERVIEW

$16.99 / $22.99 CAN

978-1-61219-814-9
ebook: 978-1-61219-815-6

RUTH BADER GINSBURG:
THE LAST INTERVIEW

$17.99 / $23.99 CAN

978-1-61219-919-1
ebook: 978-1-61219-920-7

URSULA K. LE GUIN:
THE LAST INTERVIEW

$16.99 / $21.99 CAN

978-1-61219-779-1
ebook: 978-1-61219-780-7

THE LAST INTERVIEW SERIES

JULIA CHILD:
THE LAST INTERVIEW

$16.99 / $22.99 CAN

978-1-61219-733-3
ebook: 978-1-61219-734-0

ROBERTO BOLAÑO:
THE LAST INTERVIEW

$15.95 / $17.95 CAN

978-1-61219-095-2
ebook: 978-1-61219-033-4

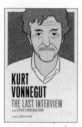

KURT VONNEGUT:
THE LAST INTERVIEW

$15.95 / $17.95 CAN

978-1-61219-090-7
ebook: 978-1-61219-091-4

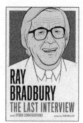

RAY BRADBURY:
THE LAST INTERVIEW

$15.95 / $15.95 CAN

978-1-61219-421-9
ebook: 978-1-61219-422-6

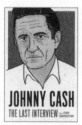

JOHNNY CASH:
THE LAST INTERVIEW

$16.99 / $22.99 CAN

978-1-61219-893-4
ebook: 978-1-61219-894-1

JAMES BALDWIN:
THE LAST INTERVIEW

$16.99 / $22.99 CAN

978-1-61219-400-4
ebook: 978-1-61219-401-1

MARILYN MONROE:
THE LAST INTERVIEW

$16.99 / $22.99 CAN

978-1-61219-877-4
ebook: 978-1-61219-878-1

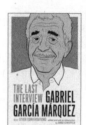

GABRIEL GARCÍA
MÁRQUEZ: THE LAST
INTERVIEW

$15.95 / $15.95 CAN

978-1-61219-480-6
ebook: 978-1-61219-481-3

THE LAST INTERVIEW SERIES

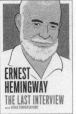

ERNEST HEMINGWAY:
THE LAST INTERVIEW

$15.95 / $20.95 CAN

978-1-61219-522-3
ebook: 978-1-61219-523-0

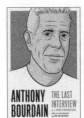

ANTHONY BOURDAIN:
THE LAST INTERVIEW

$17.99 / $23.99 CAN

978-1-61219-824-8
ebook: 978-1-61219-825-5

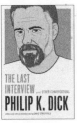

PHILIP K. DICK:
THE LAST INTERVIEW

$15.95 / $20.95 CAN

978-1-61219-526-1
ebook: 978-1-61219-527-8

MARTIN LUTHER KING, JR.:
THE LAST INTERVIEW

$15.99 / $21.99 CAN

978-1-61219-616-9
ebook: 978-1-61219-617-6

NORA EPHRON:
THE LAST INTERVIEW

$15.95 / $20.95 CAN

978-1-61219-524-7
ebook: 978-1-61219-525-4

CHRISTOPHER HITCHENS:
THE LAST INTERVIEW

$15.99 / $20.99 CAN

978-1-61219-672-5
ebook: 978-1-61219-673-2

DAVID BOWIE:
THE LAST INTERVIEW

$16.99 / $22.99 CAN

978-1-61219-575-9
ebook: 978-1-61219-576-6

HUNTER S. THOMPSON:
THE LAST INTERVIEW

$15.99 / $20.99 CAN

978-1-61219-693-0
ebook: 978-1-61219-694-7

THE LAST INTERVIEW SERIES

BILLIE HOLIDAY:
THE LAST INTERVIEW

$16.99 / $22.99 CAN

978-1-61219-674-9
ebook: 978-1-61219-675-6

KATHY ACKER:
THE LAST INTERVIEW

$16.99 / $21.99 CAN

978-1-61219-731-9
ebook: 978-1-61219-732-6

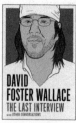

DAVID FOSTER WALLACE:
THE LAST INTERVIEW

$16.99 / $21.99 CAN

978-1-61219-741-8
ebook: 978-1-61219-742-5

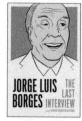

JORGE LUIS BORGES:
THE LAST INTERVIEW

$15.95 / $15.95 CAN

978-1-61219-204-8
ebook: 978-1-61219-205-5

PRINCE:
THE LAST INTERVIEW

$16.99 / $22.99 CAN

978-1-61219-745-6
ebook: 978-1-61219-746-3

HANNAH ARENDT:
THE LAST INTERVIEW

$15.95 / $15.95 CAN

978-1-61219-311-3
ebook: 978-1-61219-312-0

JANE JACOBS:
THE LAST INTERVIEW

$15.95 / $20.95 CAN

978-1-61219-534-6
ebook: 978-1-61219-535-3

LOU REED:
THE LAST INTERVIEW

$15.95 / $15.95 CAN

978-1-61219-478-3
ebook: 978-1-61219-479-0